FIRESIDE

MASTERING

Strumming, Fingerpicking, and a View of

GUITAR

Classical Guitar Technique ●

DAVID ALZOFON ●

A Fireside Book ●
Published by Simon and Schuster

10 9 8 7 6 5 4 3 2 1

Library of Congress Cataloging in Publication Data

Alzofon, David.
   Mastering guitar.

   (A Fireside book)
   1. Guitar—Methods. I. Title.
MT582.A52   787.6'1'0712   80-24682
ISBN 0-671-25421-9

Acknowledgments

It is a pleasure to acknowledge the editorial assistance of Jan Mattox, a composer, and Rani Cochran, a classical guitar instructor at San Francisco State University. Jan's imagination and enthusiasm were a steady source of inspiration to me, her criticisms extremely valuable and constructive. Rani's authoritative technical counseling was an invigorating influence, not to mention quite indispensable. My thanks also to Dr. Ronda Davé, whose keen ear for instructional language and intelligent criticisms were greatly beneficial.

I wish to express my heartfelt appreciation to Howard Roberts, jazz guitarist and teacher of wide renown, for his warm encouragement in the earliest phases of this work. Beyond that, Howard's inimitable style and personality were pricelessly inspirational.

Methods, concepts, and characters in this book were all enriched by my experiences in martial arts. Mr. H. Nishiyama, karate master, and Mr. Frank Doran, aikido instructor—also Dr. E. Flores-Magón and Dr. Martin Weiner—were particularly inspirational and influential, and I would like to thank them sincerely.

Richard Stover, an expert on Latin American history, culture, and music, was most kind in providing me with reference material. More than that, his wizardly performances of guitar works by Barrios, Lauro, and others fired my imagination.

I am deeply grateful to Jim Crockett, publisher of *Guitar Player* magazine, as well as Don Menn, Tom Mulhern, and Jerry Martin, all of *GP*, for their gracious and invaluable assistance, without which the book would surely never have achieved its present form.

A special debt of gratitude is owed to Jan McAllister for the many occasions on which she readily and generously lent her photographic expertise to the enterprise.

Many friends along the way contributed excellent suggestions, praise and criticism, as well as supporting words during the inevitable spells of pessimism and doubt, and I wish to thank them one and all for their kindness.

And finally, with great love, I thank my parents, whose wholehearted encouragement helped me immeasurably over the years it took to carry this idea into reality.

To Barbara

Contents

Introduction

Here is a guitar primer that's a little different—it's a story, too. The story's about a college student from the USA named Alfonso Fegoni and what happens when he meets up with an old eccentric named Diego de Luna, down in Venezuela. What it all has to do with guitar will become clear very shortly, so we shall say no more about it until we've given the guitar course a proper introduction. A guitar course always feels naked unless covered by an introductory word or two.

The instruction ahead is aimed at the total beginner or the somewhat experienced beginner who wants to learn to read music. As you read the story you will find assignments emerging in the dialogue. They can escape you if you're engrossed in the narrative, so to alert you we've put in a ● whenever one of these embedded assignments occurs. When you see this symbol, reread the dialogue preceding it and do what Diego de Luna has asked Alfonso Fegoni to do before you go on.

How long will it take, and what will you get out of it? Well, let's compare the course to a mountaineering expedition. There are three peaks in the range you will climb, like the three parts of this book.

Each peak should take about two weeks to conquer, making for a six-week expedition on the average. This is not one of those books that take you down complicated bypaths on your way to an uncertain destination. It's going to be like backpacking, just step by step up to the top of the mountain.

And what are these peaks? Part One gets you strumming. You will get into syncopated Latin-sounding rhythms right away, and we think you'll find it easy—even if you've never played before.

By the top of the second peak (the end of Part Two), you'll have the basics of fingerpicking down. The skills you learn will greatly smooth your entry into folk, blues, or ragtime fingerpicking styles.

On the trek up the third peak you will gather a view of the realm of classical guitar technique.

There are no abrupt transitions between parts—it's all one path. Sight-reading skill, for example, accumulates throughout all three. By the end of Part Three, if you've taken every step without cutting corners, your beginner's legs will be strong. You'll be able to move out into the other method books which seem to take so much knowledge for granted; you'll be able to learn faster when somebody shows you something; and, most important, you'll be on your way to becoming an expressive player.

This book doesn't say everything there is to say about the guitar —no book does that. This book just makes getting over those difficult first hurdles a whole lot easier, and no other book has approached them with quite the same originality. But, of course, we owe that to Diego de Luna.

One thing left out is a lecture on how to tune your guitar. So many other books give this subject a good working over and, since it is a difficult matter to communicate in words alone, we thought it better not to include it. But in Appendix A (pg. 185) you will find an illustration showing the pitches, by piano keys, to which each string is tuned, and a brief explanation of tuning by unisons. (And what a 'unison' is, too.)

And now that we have some idea of where we are going, there's no reason we shouldn't get under way. (Better tune your guitar because things are going to start moving as soon as you turn the page.)

As we join Alfonso Fegoni he is . . . well, you'd expect him to be behind a lectern, clearing his throat, ready to pontificate—at least, that's what you'd expect if you knew him. But to tell the truth, he is sneaking through the viny thicket of a Venezuelan mountain forest. And (something of a first for a guitar manual) our hero is thinking nothing of the guitar at all. Rather, he is plotting to commit burglary in the house of a senile old man.

Alfonso, I leave it to you to explain this embarrassing set of circumstances.

—David Alzofon
February, 1980

PART ONE
●
THE FIRST REALM
OF GUITAR KNOWLEDGE

LESSON I:

Encounter in Venezuela

i. A Captive Audience

It was the first time I, Alfonso Fegoni, had ever been a burglar. And it would have been an inconceivable role for me only hours earlier. I was always known to my friends as a serious, reserved student of chemistry, courteous and polite in the extreme. How, then, did this sudden transformation take place?

It all goes back to a party in the United States a month before. The University of Venezuela, Caracas, had accepted me with honors for its master's program in chemical engineering and my friends were bidding me bon voyage. At the party I met Melinda Vossinovsky, a pretty, young musicologist, who suggested I visit the countryside and tape-record some authentic folk musicians for her.

I was already a dabbler with the guitar—thought I was good, in fact, though I was kind of a closet guitarist. Drunk (a rare event), and deliriously pleased with her and with myself at the moment, I agreed.

But on a sweltering Venezuelan afternoon several thousand miles from her pretty face I began to rue that promise. My schedule was far busier than I had anticipated, and Melinda could hardly have known how difficult the little matter of finding, much less recording, the folk musicians could possibly be. I swore that this would be the last foray into the field I would make for her as I stopped in for an ice-cold beer at a seedy-looking café.

The place was nearly empty and the bartender and I struck up a conversation. When he heard what I was doing he suggested I visit a certain Diego de Luna, a *gran guitarrista*.

"He is a great *guitarrista*, maybe the best, but a little crazy," said the bartender.

"The best in your town?"

"*En el mundo*," he replied with a proud smile.

I admit that I was more than a little skeptical of the good fellow's judgment. I was tired and the beer had made me sleepy. Still, there was a chance old 'don' Diego ("Be respectful," the bartender cautioned me) could add a song or two to my collection. Besides, I really couldn't pass up a chance to meet The Greatest Guitarist In The World. Who would have expected to find him in a rural backwater of Venezuela?

The bartender's directions led me to a high stone wall that marked the boundary of the estate where Diego de Luna worked as a gardener ("When not concertizing in Paris and London," I remarked to myself). The grounds were evidently rather expansive; all that could be seen beyond the gate were the forested contours of the steep mountain ridge which encircled the town like the walls of an enormous crater. A half hour later I was perhaps a mile deep into the woods and convinced I had taken a wrong turn or, worse yet, was completely lost. The shadows had become dark and eerie under the forest canopy. The native birds warbled, chirped, chattered and croaked in the sea of foliage. But then, through the mass of trees, nestled in a clearing, I spied a cabin perfectly fitting the bartender's description.

As I approached the edge of the forest, a patch of color caught my attention. It was an overstuffed armchair in the yard on the sunny side of the cabin. Slouched in the chair, his bare feet propped up on a stump, was an old man. Turbulent snarls of gray and white hair swept back like a lion's mane from his high, brown forehead.

Even from a distance there was a sphinx-like aura about him. He sat in perfect stillness, yet whether he was relaxed or not, I couldn't tell. His face was a mix of the refined features of a European and the noble character of an Indian, angular, with prominent cheekbones.

"But is this really Diego de Luna, the gardener?" I thought, taking note of the jungle of weeds blocking my path and surrounding the cabin. "Let us hope his guitar technique is nothing like his green thumb." And with that I stepped forth into the sunlight.

When my noisy passage through the dry grass did not disturb him I began to fear he had been overcome by the sun. Hat in hand I leaned forward for a closer look, but his expression was made a riddle by the pair of coal-dark sunglasses on his nose.

Abruptly, without turning his head, he raised his hand to his mouth. A cigar was wedged between the fingers.

"Got a light, señor?" came the gruff voice.

I was a bit startled. I quickly patted around for my matches.

"Diego de Luna, *a sus órdenes*," he said, finally turning to me as I extended him the flame.

Our conversation continued in Spanish.

"You shouldn't go sneaking up on a man that way in this part of the country. Very dangerous—you could get shot, you young pup! Shot dead, just like that." He spit.

The bartender had warned me the old man was crazy—if only he had specified paranoid, I would have stayed away.

"Don Diego, you misunderstand. I wasn't sure you were awake and I didn't want to . . ."

"Don't tell me I don't understand! Sleeping in the sun? Who would sleep in the sun around here? Do you take me for a fool?"

"No, I . . ."

"It's you young people who don't understand! I've been around and I'm telling you for your own good—there's a lot of *loco hombres* in these woods. And on the streets too—everywhere, in fact! Greedy people, mad about money. Why, they wouldn't hesitate to kill you for . . . for your tennis shoes. They'd kill you for your stinking sweat socks, young man, I tell you the truth. You have to watch your step. Hey! Careful where you throw that match!"

"Sorry."

"This garden is dry as tinder this time of year!"

The match, of course, had become cold long before I discarded it.

"What did you say your name was?"

"Uh, Alfonso, Alfonso Fegoni, I'm a . . ."

"Fegoni, Fegoni . . . you have relatives in Caracas perhaps?"

"No, not that I . . ."

"Must be another Fegoni. Well, don't just stand there, you make me uncomfortable. Here, have a seat on this stump and state your business."

He kicked his feet off the stump with a grunt and motioned with his cigar. Thinking of my clean slacks I began to inspect the wood.

"Oh go on, ninny! There are no cockroaches around here—I ate the last one for breakfast this morning. What have you got in the knapsack? Any food? Any wine?"

The smile evaporated off his face like alcohol off a hot Bunsen burner when I said "tape recorder." He was up like a shot, towering over me where I sat on the stump.

"You're a *norteamericano*, aren't you!"

"Well, yes. You see . . ."

"A gringo, eh? I knew it right off! The accent, it was a dead give-away."

"I don't know if I'd call myself a . . ."

"And you've heard that I play guitar, no?"

"Yes, they say in town that you're very good."

"And so you've come to tape-record my guitar playing, no?!"

"No, I mean, yes. You see . . ."

"And then you take it back to the United States with you, eh?"

"Yes. I have a friend there who would be very pleased to hear your music . . ."

But Diego de Luna was frowning at the horizon, chewing his cigar, obviously no longer listening.

"I knew they'd come sooner or later," he muttered to himself. Then he turned to me.

"OK, señor Talent Scout, I'm old, but I'm no country bumpkin you can exploit for nothing! You tell your capitalist pig bosses 30 percent of the gross, or it's no deal . . . *comprende?!*"

"But don Diego, I'm not a talent scout!"

"You're not?"

"No, I've been trying to tell you that I . . ."

"Look, I'll go for 15 percent, but not a penny less. There's no point in bargaining, that's my bottom offer."

"Don Diego, I wish I could help you, but I am merely a university lecturer, a chemist."

Don Diego sat down and looked at me earnestly, beseechingly.

"Look, if you're going to put me in an album, you will give me credit, won't you? That's all I ask, that you spell my name correctly, *D - i - e - g - o* . . ."

"Don Diego, really, it's only for a girl friend."

The light finally seemed to dawn on him. There was a bewildered look on his face. His mouth moved but no words came out. I felt like putting a hand on the old man's shoulder, he looked so downcast. But then he began giggling, and the giggle grew into a spasmodic, wheezing and whinnying laughing fit—renewed every time he glanced my way.

However, this laughter did not seem malicious; it was rather like the kind being heard with increasing frequency on the campus back home, usually in connection with an aroma of burning herbage. I thus had the impression that he was either stoned on something or completely mad. Finally he composed himself enough to speak.

"I knew it, but I had to be sure." He extended his right hand and shook mine warmly. "It's not every day I am honored to have a man of science visit me. You are welcome here, señor Fegoni, welcome."

"Thanks," I said, more unsure than ever just where I stood.

"Say, Alfonso, do you play guitar too?"

"Well, I, er . . . uh, yes, a bit."

"*Bueno!*" he exclaimed, rising gingerly. "Come along, I want you to try my guitar."

I protested, but once inside the cottage I found a guitar pressed into my hands and a chair thrust underneath my seat. The guitar was of the fifteen-dollar class, and well worn at that.

"Play! Play!" He encouraged me with such childish eagerness I became certain of his senility. Contributing to this opinion was the wild look of his face once he removed his sunglasses. His skin was shot through with wrinkles and one of his eyes was out of line. They had a fiery gleam, like small dark garnets, and he had a habit of cocking his head slightly now and then to bring one eye or the other to bear on me. It was hard to look at him and not feel like I was staring.

"But I came to hear *you* play," I said, partly in truth and partly because I was afraid my sophisticated music would only damage the old man's pride and inhibit him.

"Oh, I'll play, but first you, I insist."

I gave in finally and began an arrangement of a song done with clever-sounding chords. I was rather proud of it. He nodded attentively with the first few beats and then began to drum his fingers nervously and to stare at the floor.

"Excuse me, amigo," he whispered. "Don't stop playing, please— I will be right back."

He departed to the kitchen, two paces away. Out of a sense of courtesy I kept playing, until at last the clatter of pots and pans made it patently absurd to continue.

De Luna came back with a plate and some silverware; he looked surprised to see that I had stopped. But without breaking stride he sat down at the table and tucked a napkin under his chin. He hummed as he adjusted things on the table.

"Don Diego?"

"Yes?" he replied crisply.

"May I ask what this is all about?"

"Eh?"

"The dinnerware?"

"Ah! Yes, yes . . . I apologize—I should've explained—but you were busy playing your music and I didn't want to interrupt. But now you've stopped—have you run out of songs already?"

"Well, I . . ."

"Oh, that's all right, I understand. Perfectly all right, no need to make excuses."

"OK," I answered, suppressing my temper.

"Now, try to understand *me.* I will explain. You see, I was getting so hungry sitting there, I couldn't think. I was getting weak, you know, my stomach—very sensitive. An old man like me has to pay attention to these things—so much as a draft in your ear while you sleep and—whiff!—like a candle, you're out! So what did I do? I went in and fixed up the kitchen. Don't bother to thank me, I think it's only right I should do that much. After you fix dinner, then I will play the guitar for you."

"Huh? What do you want?"

"Empanadas! And for dessert—my heart is set on fried bananas. Mmmmh—what a delightful dish they are!" He wagged his chin and smacked his lips.

"Now, don Diego, now . . . just wait a minute," I said with controlled calm as I put aside his guitar and came to my feet.

"Well, all right, I'll wait. But I've been waiting all afternoon for a good cook to come along and the effort has given me a hunger like el Diablo himself."

"With all due respect to you and your, uh, hospitality, don Diego, I only came here this afternoon to chat a bit and hear you play your guitar. Asking me to cook? Well it's rather out of my line, you see. And, uh, speaking of that, I notice that it is getting late in the afternoon, and so I hope you'll understand if I go now."

He had been regarding me in pop-eyed consternation throughout my speech, now he twisted his brow in disappointment and began to flush red.

"What? You are telling me that you—a man of science, a big *norteamericano* with a lot of Yankee dollars—you are too important to help out an old scarecrow like me, on his last legs with hunger?"

"Don Diego, it's not *that*—it's not that I *won't*—I *can't*. Empanadas, fried bananas—I don't even know the ingredients, much less how to cook those things. To tell you the truth, I've never cooked anything in my life."

I mustered my self-control to speak patiently with him, considering all the while the quickest way out of the situation. But at my reply a glazed look came over his eyes. Rising slowly to his feet, dropping the napkin, he was transforming before my eyes into a person possessed.

"That's it, Alfonso. . . . You've seen it—you've seen into the heart of the matter," he beamed.

As he spoke he stepped forward, and I noticed the fork still clutched in his hand. I took a step backward and around the table. I was sure he could hear my heart pounding against my chest.

"You hit upon it precisely, señor Fegoni! Yes! Of course you can't cook if you don't know the ingredients! Your insight is a better omen than I could have hoped for." He was leaning over the table almost face to face and waving the fork under my nose.

"Alfonso, you may stay, and I will teach you to cook dishes undreamed of in your science!"

He turned to laugh, or to put down his fork, or to pick up his guitar—I don't know which, because I instantly bolted for the door.

"Señor Fegoni! Where are you going? Wait! There is more!" I heard him cry.

But I didn't stop until I reached the gate at the bottom of the path. With chest heaving and my heart bursting I leaned against the cool stone wall. Then I realized my portable tape recorder, worth a small fortune—it was back there, in the cabin.

ii. The First Task of an Apprentice Guitarist

Now it should be clear how I came to be lurking about in the Venezuelan undergrowth, sweating a cold sweat. I had returned to see if I could burgle back my tape recorder and be gone. I little knew that this bizarre chain of events would lead straight into the heart of my first guitar lesson with Diego de Luna.

It was dusk and there was no light in the cabin. It seemed the old man had gone. But as I considered my next move I became aware of someone or some thing crouching beside me in the bushes. My heart leapt up into my throat and I slowly turned to see who or what was beside me.

It was don Diego de Luna.

He too was regarding the cabin with considerable interest. "Shhhh," he whispered, turning to me, "I think there is a guitar in there."

My mouth moved but no words came out.

"That's right, we must keep it quiet," he said. "Come on now, time to close in. You go first."

He nudged me and, not knowing what else to do, I crept forward through the weeds toward the cabin door. Presently we had stolen inside where it was quite shadowy, and where I quite sincerely expected to have my throat cut.

"There."

He pointed to a dark corner where I saw the dim outline of a guitar.

"Watch carefully," he said, placing his hand on my shoulder. Then he stood, walked briskly to the guitar and raised it respectfully to his chest. The harmony of his gestures was strangely hypnotic. He took a few casual steps toward me.

"You cannot betray any lack of confidence, Alfonso. She will resist you at every turn. She is not one to yield her charms easily to anyone."

He began to caress the guitar, running his hands over the neck and body, testing the strings soundlessly.

"Yes, you must assert yourself, but gently. Warm her to your touch, and only then do you play her."

Suddenly his hands blurred over the strings. The cabin reverberated with a spellbinding barrage of sonic fireworks. Then, just as suddenly, it was quiet again and de Luna's glistening black eyes surveyed me through the shadows (though I wasn't exactly sure which eye had me in its focus).

"It is your turn to play again," he declared softly and held out the guitar to me.

"But I can't . . . I can't possibly."

"You must try."

"I can't! I can't play a guitar like that! No one can play a guitar like that!"

"It is true, true you cannot play like I play. You cannot play like Diego de Luna because you are not Diego de Luna. You can only play a guitar like you. That is much better than playing like me. One must play from the heart or it is not playing, not true playing at all. Now, that is what I want you to see if you can do."

"But what *do* you want me to do, don Diego?"

"I want to see you use that guitar to liberate your spirit. That is what you want, or what you need to do—but I cannot do it for you."

"Yes, no—but it's impossible. I can't do that, not without years of practice."

Don Diego smiled. His expression was ironic, but considerate.

"Nonsense! It will be your first assignment, as well as your last. Take this guitar. Go on, take it. Now play it, and let it be played with the power of your spirit."

I took the guitar in my hands. When I plunked hesitantly at the strings the wood hummed warmly against my chest. It was a more responsive guitar than any I had ever experienced.

Don Diego took a chair across the room and lit a cigar in the shadows. His expression, illuminated by the ember, was distant—hard to define—yet this was encouraging somehow. He no longer looked at me at all. In effect I was alone with the guitar.

I began to play—cautiously, haltingly at first, single notes and single chords. Then I picked a phrase or two from things I had memorized. These sounded flat. I let them go, discarding them instinctively as I began to feel a force gradually rising from within the guitar itself —wavelike, surging, and uninhibited. It was as if the instrument was demanding to be played a certain way. My handling of the energy seemed awkward, inadequate—but this did not matter, the guitar was alive, burning with an ecstatic fire.

I played unselfconsciously like this for a brief while, then I began to hear the chaotic sounds I was making and to feel ridiculous. I wondered what don Diego must have thought of my laughable performance. I stopped the strings. He came over to where I sat, took the guitar from me and smiled warmly.

"Better playing by far than this afternoon, Alfonso. To say the least. Yes, you've brought out your spirit—you've shown some real feeling. The way everything wobbled around in the middle, never louder, never softer, when you played earlier, I thought you were determined to be unexciting. I wasn't sure you had it in you, and I had to set you this test. Now it pleases me to say I will welcome you as an apprentice."

Even as I began to ponder his offer in my somewhat befogged state, he went on, as if taking my agreement for granted.

"However, this means starting over, from the beginning!"

This remark raised my blood pressure. "I'm not exactly a beginner, don Diego. I've been playing for several years. I've studied several books too . . ."

"Alfonso, I am initiating you into the art as you've never known it before. Trust my judgment; to my way of thinking you are a beginner, and as a beginner you have a marvelous advantage—you don't know anything! That is, your mind is empty. Well, almost empty, and this is a highly desirable state, or so a wise man once told me and I believe it to be so."

"But don Diego, you're not being logical."

"No?" He frowned.

"Well, no. I'm an experienced player; how can you say my mind is empty?"

"But Alfonso—when you played just now you shed an old skin. True, your fingers are educated, but you will never be the same guitarist again. You are a new guitarist, newly born—is that not being a beginner?"

iii. The Basic Stuff of Guitar Knowledge

"Well, uh, don Diego . . . what do you put in the beginning, chords? I already know dozens of chords, maybe hundreds of chords."

"In the beginning is Time, Alfonso. Nothing exists before Time —not chords, I'll tell you that."

"Time?"

"Yes, you know—it flows through your foot."

"My foot?"

"Yes, I suppose you can tap your foot, eh?"

"Oh, yeah, well . . . sure I can."

"Then let us tap."

Don Diego lit a lantern and produced a little chalkboard. He made a row of marks on the board and pointed to them one after the other as he tapped.

"We're making a pulsation in time. And we call this pulse 'the beat.' I call these things 'beat markers.'

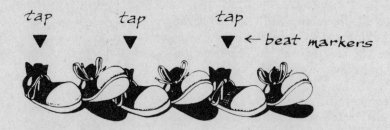

"Let's read and play this line of beat markers together, eh, Alfonso? Sing 'La-La-La-La-La,' as you read along. ●

"Good, Alfonso. Now group the taps by accenting the first of every two. Let's do that for a while.

"Now let's accent the first of every third beat.

"Yes, Alfonso, be sure to read the beat markers as you vocalize.
"Now, please accent the first in each group of four. ●

"Excellent. Now we're going to do these again, but this time I want you to use your whole body to express the beat. A restraint in your body is a restraint on your spirit. Sway with it—slap your hands on your knees to accent the first beat.

"Vigorously, Alfonso! Please," he added quietly with his finger raised, "no restraint." ●

"Much better, much. Now this is how we show the grouping of beats." As he spoke the chalk went clicking over the board.

"The number of beats per group is given by a time signature—a number at the beginning of the line of music. The beginning of a new group of beats is shown by a vertical line called a bar-line.

time signature   bar lines

4 ▼ ▼ ▼ ▼ | ▼ ▼ ▼ ▼ | ▼ ▼ ▼ ▼ | ▼ ▼ ▼ ▼ ‖

measures

Double bar
means "end."

"The pattern of beats—accented once every two, or once every three, or whatever—is called 'meter.' Each bar-line begins a new 'measure,' a new group of beats in the pattern. Meter *means* measure, Alfonso—a measure of oats, a measure of barley, or a measure of beats. *Comprende?"* *

"Yes, don Diego."

Now, how many measures have I written here? Four? And how many bars? Four again, Alfonso? You are correct.

"So, if I asked you how long this piece of music was, what would you tell me?"

"Four measures? Or maybe four bars?"

"Either one, either one. Very good."

iv. *To Stroke or Not to Stroke*

Don Diego brought out another guitar.

"Let us make use of this ability to shape the flow of time, Alfonso. Please, take this guitar. May I suggest this playing position? It is comfortable and the left foot is free to tap-tap-tap, eh?

"Good. Now relax, but don't slouch. One must guard against taking on the stage presence of a wilted poppy! The musical spirits are choosy about their mediums, you know, Alfonso.

"Now your hand, your right hand. Extend the thumb, and curl the wrist slightly too—think of a cat pawing some yarn.

"Good. Try shaking your hand from the wrist. ●

"Fine. Now use a similar wrist motion to stroke the strings with your thumb. Stroke only on the downward motion—like this:

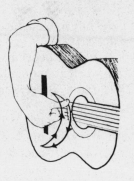

"Start slow, very slow, then speed up. Use your hand just as if you were flicking away some pesty insect. But try for a soft, smooth and even sound.

* *Definitions will accompany all musical terms used in the text, but it would be very worthwhile to invest in a music dictionary at some point in the future. Pocket Books publishes a good one—*The Harvard Brief Dictionary of Music, *by Willi Apel and Ralph T. Daniel—in paperback.*

"Good, good! Now start your foot tapping—tapping and stroking in time." ●

Don Diego called a halt and raised his finger to emphasize a point.

"The mind is quick to see the goal, but the body is like a burro that must be coaxed and prodded every step of the way. A lazy, reluctant burro. Therefore, though I am sure you understand this technique very well with your mind and probably feel it is a very simple matter, I want you to coax your body too into such a deep understanding by playing continuous downstrokes for a while more. . . . Good. Try stroking the strings only every *other* beat. Now pay attention—you must keep time on the silent beats by making a catch-stroke with the hand. I mean the hand jerks to the beat, but does not contact the strings, does not make a sound. Watch: STROKE, catch, STROKE, catch, STROKE, and so on, *comprende?* ●

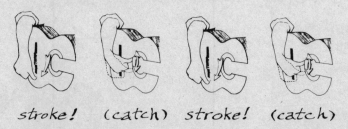

stroke! (catch) stroke! (catch)

"Your attention will wander. This is natural. When it does, bring it back to the sound. The sound, the sound, the sound! Think of its quality, its volume, its overall consistency—become a master of these three. This is much more difficult than you think. That is why this exercise is not so elementary after all! Do you understand what I want you to do?"

"I think so. It seems clear—play every beat for a while, then, maintaining the tempo, play only every other beat, right?"

"Yes, right. Please, make music! . . . Ah, too fast, amigo. Be slow, deliberate, smooth."

"Too fast!? I thought I was going too slow."

"Ah, you have not been in this part of Venezuela long enough, my *norteamericano* friend, to know what slow is yet. Make it flow like cold honey, for I want you to feel the pleasure of being in control." There was a note of irony on the word 'control.'

Don Diego called me on a minor point as soon as I started.

"Alfonso—even at a slow tempo one must swing one's hand with a fast, flicking motion. Do not drag your thumb so-as-to-hear-e-ve-ry-string."

Then I saw the reason for don Diego's ironic tone. It really was harder to space the strokes evenly at a very slow tempo. But I found it helpful to keep my hand moving in a slow, steady circle after the fast, flicking stroke. ●

When I got better at keeping time don Diego allowed me to speed up. Then the catch-stroke was added. Before too long I could feed them in without a thought. ●

"Now try grouping the beats as before. Accent the first of two. Keep it up a while. ●

"Good. Now three: One-two-three, One-two-three! ●

"Try accenting the first of every four now. ●

"I'm writing out the exercise with the catch-stroke here. This symbol ▼ means a downstroke. And this ▽ means a catch-stroke, a silent beat, in other words."

"Why all this bother about making silent beats?" I asked.

"Patience, Alfonso, please—as an old man I am entitled to take my time about coming to the point.

"Right now I'd like you to try reading this exercise as you play. Get used to reading one measure ahead. Also, do not indulge in looking at your hands—rely on a feeling for the strings. ●

4 ▼ ▼ ▼ ▽ | ▼ ▽ ▼ ▽ | ▼ ▼ ▼ ▽ | ▼ ▽ ▽ ▽ ‖

"Here are some others:" ●

a. 4 ▼ ▼ ▼ ▼ | ▼ ▼ ▽ ▽ | ▼ ▼ ▽ ▽ | ▼ ▽ ▽ ▽ ‖

b. 3 ▼ ▼ ▼ | ▼ ▽ ▽ | ▼ ▼ ▼ | ▼ ▽ ▽ ‖

c. 4 ▼ ▽ ▼ ▼ | ▽ ▽ ▼ ▼ | ▼ ▽ ▼ ▼ | ▼ ▽ ▽ ▽ ‖

d. 3 ▼ ▼ ▼ | ▼ ▽ ▼ | ▼ ▼ ▼ | ▼ ▽ ▽ ‖

e. 4 ▼ ▽ ▼ ▼ | ▼ ▽ ▼ ▼ | ▼ ▽ ▼ ▽ | ▼ ▽ ▽ ▽ ‖

f. 3 ▼ ▼ ▼ | ▼ ▼ ▽ | ▼ ▽ ▼ | ▼ ▽ ▽ ‖

v. To Pin the Shadow of a Chord

Don Diego passed me a handkerchief. "You've worked up quite a sweat."

"It's the climate. I'm not used to it."

"The air-conditioning here leaves something to be desired," he said, opening a shutter (which drained at least a portion of the cigar smoke from the room).

This remark, as well as others, caused me to reflect suspiciously on don Diego's sophistication and subtlety. His behavior could be bizarre, his thinking irrational and delusionary; he was subject to wild changes in mood—but he was not stupid. And at least one part of his mind, the part concerned with guitar playing, was highly ordered. He was clearly capable of deception, and he seemed to project this trait on the world around him. A course I had taken in abnormal psychology provided me with the clinical diagnosis—paranoid schizophrenia—and a fascinating specimen at that. Probably a little senile dementia in his makeup as well.

The scene we had played out earlier began to take on some clarity now—"Obviously he is trying to induct me into his delusionary world. That is what 'apprenticeship' really means." Feeling that I had seen the truth of the situation, I went on with the lesson fully on my guard. But I still could not fathom whatever was in don Diego's eyes; in fact, I had the uneasy sensation that the reverse was happening.

"It is partly the climate that makes you sweat, Alfonso, but, you must learn to relax more. You are tense—tense. You are always analyzing. Your brain works too hard—that's the problem. Relax and you'll do better. Take a few deep breaths now. Just relax, my friend—if you have a disciplined mind, then show me by relaxing it, eh?" ●

Don Diego smiled and, along with me, took a few deep breaths and stretched a bit. "Do you feel better now?" he asked, puffing on a new cigar.

"Yes much better."

Well, of course I did—a few deep breaths always does relax one somewhat. Besides, I had seen right through this effort to disarm me another step, and for that I felt rather clever.

"Well then, what now? Ah, let us focus on the left hand. Chords —we'll learn some chords. Now a chord is a group of three or more notes chosen for their harmony. What might that mean to you, as a guitar player?"

"That I'll have to get my left hand fingers down on several strings at the same time?"

"Sí. And part of the problem of learning chords is remembering where to put your fingers."

"Oh sure, that's what chord charts are for."

"Chord charts, eh?"

"I know lots of them."

"Forget them."

"Forget them?"

"You must use . . . the shadow of the chord."

"What is the shadow of the chord?"

"Well, a chart by itself *(see drawing)* is a shadow image of the strings and frets, isn't it?"

"Yes, so it is."

"Now if your fingertips made shadows where they touched the strings, they would give you the *shadow of the chord*. For example, here is E major, and now, here is the shadow . . . and the chart of the chord."

"You see, Alfonso, the problem with memorizing a chord chart is that the same chord can be fingered several different ways, and the way you memorize may not be the best."

"Yeah, but if I had the right charts . . ."

"There are no right charts. The right way to finger a chord is the

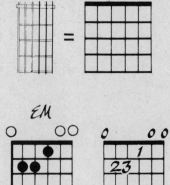

o = open string note.

way that allows you to go smoothly into it and out of it. Thus the 'right' fingering varies."

"Oh, I see."

"Later, when you use the shadow of the chord for other things, you will fully appreciate the value of the idea. Right now you can see that a shadow is a simpler thing to remember than three different chord charts, and you will also find that when your fingers have a shadow to pin down, then they find their place much more quickly."

"A-ha."

"When you have a new chord, try pinning the shadow, or even small parts of the shadow, in different ways. The chords will remain in your mind forever after that . . ."

"Like peanut butter," I said, while, as I watched in awe, he played a brilliant series of rapid-fire chords.

"Of course you'd like to play better, Alfonso—why, even I would like to play better . . ."

"No, I said . . ."

"Just put your trust in me, Alfonso, my friend—and keep your seat glued to the practice chair—you'll make a decent player in no time."

"Yes, don Diego."

"Make the E major chord now. Good. Pay close attention to the sensations coming from the skin surfaces in contact with each other. Memory of this will aid you in gathering your fingers into the right shape before they even touch the strings. The grip should be firm, but *flexible*, eh? Try wobbling your hand in little circles while keeping the fingertips firmly pressing." ●

"About the thumb . . ."

"Yes, it is better to place the thumb pad flat against the neck of the guitar."

"Rather than what?"

"Rather than clasping the neck in the palm of the hand. If I did that (*see right*) it would give my fingers trouble."

"What kind of trouble?"

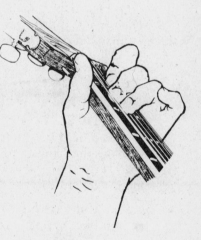

"Clasping the neck would make it difficult for my fingers to attack the strings as straight up and down as possible."

"Why exactly do you want the fingers to be straight up and down?"

"More strength! That, and because they're less inclined to inter-fere with a neighboring string when straight up and down."

"If they're straight up and down they are 'less inclined' indeed, right, don Diego?"

But he didn't seem to catch my play on words. He stared distract-edly at me a second and went right on to another subject. I wondered if the man had any sense of humor.

vi. Elementary Coordination

"Where was I . . . ah yes. Here is another chord for you, Alfonso—A minor. It has the same shadow as E major, notice, but over one set of strings.

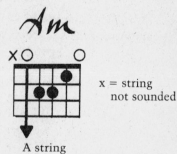

x = string
not sounded

A string

"*Puf!* Mud! Mud!"

"What?"

"Begin the stroke on string 5, please, Alfonso. Avoid hitting string 6 or the sound will be very ugly."

"Sounds OK to me."

"Someday, Alfonso, you will have ears for sounds as a winetaster has tastebuds for wines—and then you will know—it is a most distasteful vibration to mix the sounds of these strings."

"Oh."

"Now E major progresses well to A minor and vice versa. Thus you have your first chord progression at hand."

"Progression?"

"—A series of chords, a parade, if you like."

It struck me as peculiar that a man who scoffed at learning from books was giving every indication of knowing the book-learned vocabulary. First "meter," and now "progression." But then again, maybe he picked up such words on the street somehow. Trying to gather more clues, I tuned in closely on what he was saying.

"Please, try switching back and forth between E major and A minor while strumming." ●

*ad lib: at the player's discretion

"Hmm . . . the strings are buzzing, don Diego."

"Stop strumming, but hold the chord. Now test each string."

"A-ha," I said, "it's the fourth string."

"Then move your finger closer to the fret crossed by the fourth string. It may not even be necessary to press harder."

 best pressure point

"That did it, don Diego."

"A good procedure—to test each string. But sometimes one must simply shake the hands loose and this restores strength and responsiveness.

Don Diego wrote out an exercise and held it up for inspection.

"The last chord is held for two beats and two beats only," he pointed out.

"Stop the strings after the second beat by resting your hand against them near the bridge. Here, use the thumbside edge of the hand, not the palm." ●

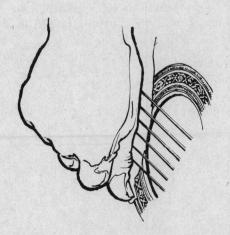

"There is a challenge in this next exercise," de Luna said.

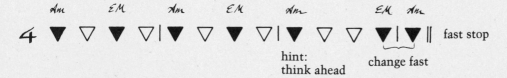

"What's the challenge? It looks easy."

"The challenge is to keep from slowing down between measures three and four."

"Because of the chord change?"

"Correct. Also, you must let the last chord ring for only one beat. It will tax your speed and dexterity to do these things well and smoothly."

"It still looks easy," I said as I began to strum. ●

True to my feeling, I got the exercise under control in short order, but don Diego encouraged me to repeat it over and over, without stopping—and as I did he began a quiet but intricate accompaniment punctuated by a slap across the fretboard now and then. When he caught me staring at his hands, he stopped immediately.

"Was I interfering, Alfonso?"

"No, don Diego, it was beautiful . . . what you were doing. How . . . I mean, can you explain how that is done?"

With a detached air, don Diego began to explain.

"Well, you see, if I apply the heel of my palm to the strings at choice moments it is, how shall I say?—like a provocative hesitation in the breath?"

"I don't get you. What do you mean?"

"I mean it is, what is the word? Ah, 'sexy.' Does that make sense to you? But of course, if you'd like to learn it, you will have to study the silent beat, and I seem to recall you saying that was a bothersome subject."

"Bothersome? Uh, no—I think I just said I wanted to know why it was so important."

"Ah, this is why it is so important! Shall I proceed?"

"By all means!"

"Alfonso, you are living proof that curiosity is natural to the scientific mind. Commendable, very commendable."

vii. *The Art of Offbeat Thinking*

De Luna gestured at his foot and began to tap. The dust rose in puffs from his bare wooden floor.

"Observe," he said. "Foot-tapping has an upstroke as well as a downstroke, just as breath has 'inhale' as well as 'exhale.' "

"The downstroke on guitar or foot-tapping—that's the *beat.*"

"*Sí.*"

"The upstroke . . . is the *offbeat!*

"We'll make an upside-down arrowhead for the offbeat. Now let's count as we tap—one-and, two-and . . . ●

one - and - two - and - three - and - and so on

"And to make it easier to see the grouping of beats and offbeats, we'll add stems . . . and beams:

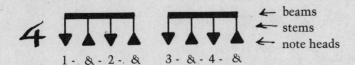

"Let's read and 'sing' along with this bar."
"I really can't sing, don Diego."
"Just a 'La–la, la–la' will do, Alfonso."
"No, really, I can't . . ."
"False modesty, my friend—together now, begin!" ●

We repeated the bar a few times with don Diego pointing out the beats as we read along, then he wiped it off the chalkboard with his fist and wrote another:

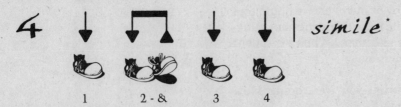

*simile (see-mee-lay); continue in a similar manner

"Only one beat is split here, Alfonso. Keep a nice 'One-two-three-four going, and double-time the 'La–la' on beat two. Try it. ●

"Well done, but I think you could stand to bring out the 'One' a little stronger. So, again, please. ●

"Here are some others. I think you would find it helpful to establish the beat as you go into the exercise bar, like this: [(a) below.] ●

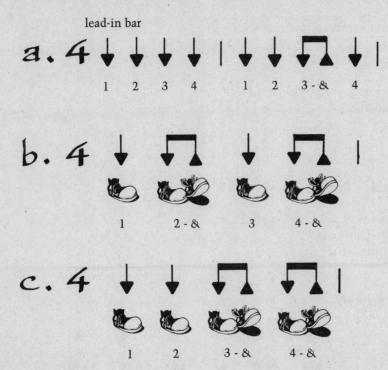

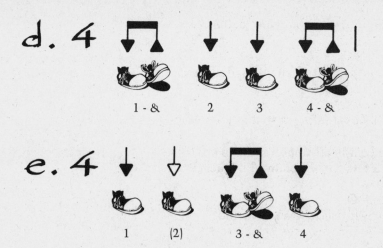

"We are one step away from making it sound Latin, Alfonso."

"Meaning sexy, don Diego?"

"Precisely, Alfonso. Now let me put a problem to you: What will it sound like if we silence a beat here or there, especially right before an off-beat?"

"I'm lost."

"Well, take this one [(a) above]. Suppose the third beat were silenced, but the offbeat sounded?"

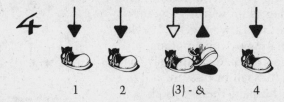

"I don't know."

"Try counting it as before—but say 'mm' to yourself instead of 'three.' The foot must keep steadily tapping out the beat."

"OK, here goes—One, two, mm-and four."

"Don't stop now—you're doing fine! Repeat, repeat—let that 'mm' get softer and softer. Let it fade out until it is just a little tightening in your throat on 'three.' But you still say 'and' with force."

"A juggling act—with the foot-tap and all."

"A lot of music is just that, Alfonso. ●

"A-ha! Now you are syncopating," he exclaimed.

"But I thought I was doing everything just as you wanted."

"*Caramba!* You did indeed do as I asked, Alfonso! Shifting the accent off the beat like this is called syn-co-PA-tion."

"You mean I was doing it right?"

"Absolutely! Now can you read this for me?

"Allow me to help. You are counting as if there were five beats to the measure. As you can see by the time signature . . ."

"There should be just four, right?"

"Yes, so on the second beat you must fit in an 'and' halfway between 'two' and 'three.' "

"Dumb mistake."

"Now don't say that, this is a new idea to you. Why don't you tackle this problem on your own now?"

"Me, huh?"

"Yes, try. And please think out loud—I'm interested in following along."

"OK, don Diego. Let's see—the beat is all-important, apparently, so first I'll set the beat. I'll tap out a few bars of plain old 'One, two, three, four.' "

"Stage One," de Luna commented. ●

"Then, keeping the beat rolling, I'll count 'One, two-and, three, four.' "

"Stage Two." ●

"Then I'll make it 'One, mm-and, three, four,' letting 'mm' fade out until I get 'One, -and, three, four.' "

"Stage Three." ●

Don Diego applauded me. "Well done," he said. "Now perfect your technique with these": (*See right.*) ●

When I started to vocalize the last rhythm don Diego picked up his guitar and began to strum along. Then I quit and he kept on playing.

I put my chin on my hand and listened as he began to spin a rather colorful yarn in song over the breezy rhythms. It went something like this: Once there was an old tub of a merchant ship whose crew loved singing and guitar playing, but whose captain was always grim. He was grim because he suspected his men of being happy for no pious, productive reason. For their own good, then, he preached ceaselessly that only through hard work could a man fulfill himself in this life and the next. To teach them the value of money, he paid them nickels and dimes and rationed their bread.

A storm came up and, because the Captain wouldn't cast off an ounce of cargo, the ship wallowed and broke into splinters. Everyone drowned and went straight to Hell, where the Devil lined them up for judgment. The Captain stepped right out and started ranting that he was there by mistake—his men were the sinners, not him! The men protested, but the Devil glowered at them and got the Captain to tell him about their sins in detail. "Enough," said The Wicked One presently, and pointing a menacing finger at the crew, he made them vanish.

Then the Captain pressed his advantage by enumerating all the sins he had resisted throughout his life. It was a hilarious list, but the Devil got tired of him very fast and, with a wink, sent him up to Heaven.

The Captain waited in line for a hundred years or so, and finally came before the Lord.

"Ah yes, *you*," said God.

"I thought you'd know me, Lord," said the Captain, "for I prayed an hour every day and tried to better the souls of others, as well as my own."

"Your men mentioned that in many an oath upon my Name."

"The drunken scum got just what they deserved! And all I ask, Lord, is that I get the same."

"So you shall. You prayed for wealth, now take this bag of gold

a. ↓ ↓ ↓ ↓↑

b. ↓ ↓ ↓↑↓↑↓

c. ↓ ↓ ↓↑↓↑↓

d. ↓ ↓↑ ↓ ↓↑

e. ↓ ↓↑ ↓ ↓↑

f. ↓↑↓↑ ↓ ↓↑

g. ↓ ↓↑ ↓↑↓↑↓

h. ↓ ↓↑ ↓↑↓↑↓

i. ↓ ↓↑ ↓↑↓↑↓

j. ↓ ↓↑ ↓↑↓↑↓

bricks . . . and take this hammer and go forth to repair the streets of Heaven, in order that your soul by hard work may continue to be improved."

"What?!"

"And after that—we'll discuss the roofs."

What about the crew? Well, the Devil had been so impressed with the Captain's account of them that he had sent them back to Earth, as rich men, to maintain the good work.

The last refrain ended and de Luna began to improvise melodies with his voice. I was completely caught up by this time tapping my foot and nodding my head. But then something snapped me out of it, an awareness of the isolation of this lantern-lit room and the very strange and unpredictable old man who was singing this song.

"What's the matter? You don't like my calypso, Alfonso?"

"Why no . . . I mean *yes*, I liked your calypso. It was splendid."

"I thought I saw you make a funny face like you felt a cockroach crawl down your shirt, and you stopped tapping."

I was afraid de Luna was getting paranoid again, so I tried to return his attention to the music.

"It was my nose—I . . . I have allergies. That was a very interesting song, don Diego. Is there any chance you'd teach me some of those strums?"

"Why yes, in fact I was just preparing to show you how to apply your offbeat thinking to the guitar.

viii. *Applied Offbeat Thinking*

"First we need a stroke for the offbeat. This is easily done. Stroke down with the thumb for the beat, and stroke up with the index finger for the offbeat. It's all in the wrist—like this:

"Flick the hand quickly to get the strings into action all at once."

"It reminds me of how you shake your hand when you get a burn."

"Now I have two exercises for you, one to develop your control of loudness, the other to develop your control of speed. If you do them every day, just as a warm-up, your awareness of these two vital dimensions will be greatly deepened, beyond a doubt.

"Now, for the volume: Begin by playing as soft as a whisper. Gradually raise the voice of the guitar until it is as loud as you can make it without banging the strings on the fretboard—then taper off slowly down to a whisper again. Don't rush yourself. Incidentally, we refer to the volume changes in a piece of music as *dynamics*. ●

"Now, for speed, start with the tempo of a Peruvian waltz . . ."

"What's that?"

"You don't know?"

"Uh-uh."

"But you know the samba, don't you?"

"Sorry."

"The tango?"

"No."

"*Caramba.* You must think I'm a page from an old scrapbook, eh?"

"Well, I don't dance."

"Ah, that explains it—you're the old coot."

"I've got a ways to go yet on that—I'm just 22."

"You are 22! Well, well . . . what a sorrow, Alfonso, it's worse than I thought." Don Diego smiled. I was unamused. ". . . But there's hope. Ahem, well, there are other names for a tempo, Alfonso."

"Like what?"

"Like *largo, andante, presto* . . . Are you familiar with the tempo term *prestissimo,* Alfonso?"

"Uh, no, not really."

" 'As fast as possible,' that's what it means, and that's how fast I want you to play in the middle of this exercise.

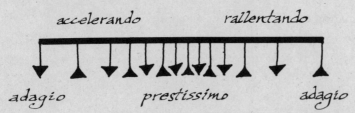

accelerando: gradually faster
adagio: slow tempo
rallentando: gradually slackening pace

"Now, as with the exercise in controlling loudness, don't hurry to your peak speed. Try to shade up to it in fine degrees.

"Good, but don't play louder, just because you are playing faster —unless you mean to?"

"Uh, no . . . I didn't think of it."

"A-ha! Your awareness does need deepening! ●

"I am sure you will have no trouble strumming offbeat rhythms in various meters now, Alfonso. Let's try a pattern in two-time. ●

"Now a pattern in waltz time. Accent the first beat!"

"I know—exaggerate it."

"It will do no harm." ●

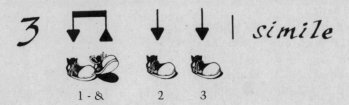

* $\blacksquare\!|\!|\!:$ and $:\!|\!|$ are *repeat marks,* meaning "repeat the enclosed material." The left-hand mark is omitted when the repeat goes back to the beginning of the piece or section.

A minute later we changed to a four-beat meter with the following rhythm pattern: ●

"You see Alfonso? You are becoming quite good at this."

"Thanks."

"Try these patterns now. They are the same ones you learned with your voice a while earlier, so, while you work on them, I will write another that will be more challenging."

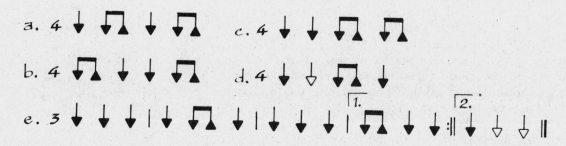

ix. Alfonso Fegoni—Syncopated Guitar Strummer

Something was gleaming in don Diego's eyes when he addressed the next subject.

"I told you it would take awhile, but prick your ears up, all right? Because now I'm going to make all the 'bother' over the silent beat pay off, and pay off well."

"Good," I said. I must have said it wearily.

"Alfonso, alert yourself, please—this is the climax of today's lesson. You have come an enormous distance tonight, and that is excellent. But it has all been but in preparation for what I am about to reveal to you. Don't let your energy fail now—for now is when you will need it most."

I straightened my sagging back and pulled the guitar into playing position.

"Good. Now let's tap and sing 'la–la–la' to this little ditty: ●

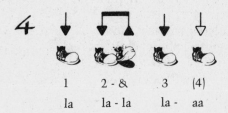

"OK. Can you strum it? Good. ●

"Now I'm going to rewrite the exercise with one small change— observe":

* ⌐1. and ⌐2. mean *first* and *second endings.* Thus in (e) play bars 1–4, repeat 1–3, skip to the second ending and stop at the double bar.

"You silenced the second beat."

"Yes."

"Syncopated it."

"Yes, yes! Let's sing it together. ●

"Good. All that remains is to play it. That means playing it as we did before, but this time *not* hitting the strings on beat two—"

"But being *sure* to catch the strings with the index finger on the upstroke half of the catch-stroke motion."

"Yes, Alfonso. As the hand dips, the thumb misses, but the first finger will hit the strings as the hand comes up. Of course, it is all one motion. And *then*, without hesitation—I emphasize—*without hesitation*, the thumb comes down for beat three. The beat must roll on undisturbed."

"OK, let me take it solo." ●

"Well, Alfonso, you handled that perfectly. I noticed you kept the tempo slow. You were in control. Very good."

Don Diego rose and stretched.

"We have reached the end of the lesson. I shall write out some exercises in syncopated strumming. It will take only a minute."

He dashed them off and handed them to me, only ten small entries on the piece of paper. (*shown at right*)

"Take them with you with my compliments. They are very easy, only one measure each. The trick is to be able to play each measure accurately, over and over, continuously. If you have trouble playing the syncopated beats, remember how we did this one."

"I notice you haven't written any lead-in bars."

"No! But play one each time you start an exercise! It is very important to set the tempo and then adhere to it."

x. *Beautiful Country, but Can You Trust the Tour Guides?*

It was after midnight when at last don Diego and I stepped out of the cabin into the fresh night air. The stars were brilliant in the unfamiliar Southern sky, and a new moon had risen. And under this vast dome, dusted with numberless sparkling lights, was the forest, looking now like a ragged black tear through the fabric of the heavens.

"Beautiful, isn't it?" said don Diego, folding his arms and smiling as if it all belonged to him and he was terribly proud of his possession.

"Yes, it's tremendous."

"What's the matter? You don't sound happy, Alfonso—can't you taste that night air?" He spread his arms wide with a deep breath, then he took a drag on his cigar. "Doesn't it fill you with a restless energy, a sense of wonder? Why, just look at those stars! Now you may know the exact chemical composition of those gleaming little points of light —they may be machines—but they are wondrous machines! So beautiful, each and every one, and all together. Ah, I know I sound like a damned tour guide, Alfonso, but I mean what I'm saying, or trying to say."

"I think it's kind of beautiful that we know their chemical composition, don Diego."

"Splendid thought, Alfonso. I don't see why, if I thought the stars were beautiful, I wouldn't find their plumbing an interesting affair as well. In all truth, Alfonso, I wish I knew their clockworks and their paths, their origins and their destinations . . ."

I rolled my eyes upward at de Luna's hopeless naiveté about science.

". . . Think how you could impress a young woman on a night such as this—when the two of you take a walk alone. Why, I wish I'd known what you know when I was a young man. Do you suppose, Alfonso, that there is life, intelligent life, out there somewhere?"

"There's a high probability."

Don Diego sighed, "I would give my eyeteeth to hear their guitar playing.

"Well, enough talking—I am sure you want to get back. The exercises should take you no more than three days to master, so let us meet back here, say, Wednesday? That is a little long, but in a while you will have the capacity to study with me every day."

"Don Diego—as I said—I am here to study at the University. It's a long ways off, and . . . well, I can't possibly return until next weekend."

"Very well, then—next weekend." He gazed off into the night and there was a silence. "You look worried, Alfonso. Did you think I would let you walk back alone?"

I was much relieved. "Thank you, don Diego, I . . . I left my flashlight back at the car."

"Flashlight? Humpf . . . *un momento.*"

Don Diego disappeared into the house. He was back not long after and the very sight of him made my blood run cold. He had on a double-breasted bullet belt, a bandolera which bristled with shells. A pistol hung from his hip, and an old rifle—possibly a Winchester—was slung on the opposite shoulder. Don Diego was a guerrilla, except for his headgear, which, strange to say, consisted of one well-worn baseball cap—The Yankees.

Smiling at me cockeyed and confident as he passed he said, "Come on, amigo, I'll see you back safe and sound."

As he struck off for the forest I followed in his footsteps, full of dread.

Don Diego had no light. He insisted it would attract bandits and jaguars. Thus my progress down the slope was marked by stumbling and tripping, don Diego warning me all the while to keep quiet. I feared that he too might trip, and go off like a munitions dump when he hit the ground, but he seemed to be able to see in the dark.

When we reached the gate don Diego shook my hand and I found myself thanking him and agreeing to return the following week. I watched him go, melting like a shadow into the dark forest from which we had just emerged. Finally I was left all alone with my backpack and my tape recorder with its blank cassette still in place and the meter on zero.

I shook my head and turned around to face the street. I was confused momentarily, unable to remember where I had left the car.

"Good grief," I said, "here I am a guitar apprentice to an armed, paranoid schizophrenic lunatic!"

I got back to Caracas in the wee hours of the morning. By the time I rolled into bed I almost thought I had dreamed the whole thing.

The following morning I awoke with the scent of stale cigar smoke in my nostrils. I eased myself up in bed, noted that my legs ached, then grabbed yesterday's shirt off the covers and flung it into the closet. I fell back on the pillow. Ten A.M.—I was already late for my first appointment, an interview with Dr. Forzosa, head of the Department of Chemical Engineering.

"This Diego de Luna thing has got to be forgotten," I thought. "I am not in Venezuela to play the guitar! I have classes to attend, experiments to conduct, papers to write. How will I explain my lateness to Professor Forzosa?

"Interesting fellow, Diego de Luna—but disturbing, unpredictable. . . . Is it safe to encourage him? How would he react if I show less than complete devotion to the 'apprenticeship?' And what if I wanted to quit at some point? Imagine a man as balmy as that keeping guns around—he probably uses them on apprentices who want to leave his delusionary world.

" 'Apprenticeship'—how grandiose! It's guitar lessons. That's all it is, just guitar lessons. He does seem to have some sophistication, on musical matters anyway. I wonder what his background is? Oh well, what does it matter?

"Cripes, that cigar smoke makes me sick!" I said as I forced myself out of bed and staggered to the bathroom.

My mind was still in a fog when I stepped out into the glaring daylight and began the walk to school a half hour later. Someone jostled me on the sidewalk as I strolled along deep in thought, but I scarcely noticed. Then two or three more people rudely brushed past at a good clip.

"Hey, watch where you're going!" I turned and shouted.

When I turned back I was facing a mob of stampeding young men and women that had suddenly begun pouring from a side street nearby. They were bearing down on me at a gallop, screaming and shouting chaotically. A smoking projectile arched over their heads and clattered in the street.

Tear gas?

When another and another zipped up into the air and a rear guard of bobbing helmets came into view, I snapped out of my dreamy state, spun around and ran with the mob.

I took the flight of stairs to my apartment at a sprint. With singed nostrils and watering eyes, I jumped into the shower.

As I was flushing my eyes and thinking what an unfortunate morning it had been for fragrances (cigar smoke is infinitely preferable to tear gas, I concluded), the phone rang.

It was a very fretful Professor Forzosa. My failure to appear on campus had alarmed him, but after being reassured that I had not been shot or arrested, and only moderately gassed, he calmed down. In fact, his mood changed to vague irritation when he discovered I was completely unaware of the buildup of political tension over the weekend. There was an undertone of 'Where have *you* been?' in his explanation.

The riots, he said, were fomented by an insignificant clique of militant radicals and he hoped I would not form the wrong impression of the school. Most of the students were 'serious' and the situation, he assured me, would be 'normalized' by Tuesday. Meanwhile, it would be a good idea to stay off the streets. After another apology he hung up.

I went to the window. There were troops on every street corner. Military vehicles would occasionally go racing past, evidently intent on activities the journalists neatly summarize under the title 'mopping up patches of resistance.'

There seemed to be nothing to do but wait out the storm. Not having been to class I had no studying to do, so I turned to my library of science books for recreation. There were a number of them I had read only once or twice, so at least the time could be put to good use.

But after only ten minutes of the first book, I got bored.

Now this was an almost unheard of event—for me, that is. I decided the subject matter was to blame. I got another book out. And got the same reaction.

"Probably the excitement and lack of sleep," I thought.

It was then I noticed my guitar in the corner of the room. My boredom vanished on the instant.

The exercises de Luna had given me were not what I had in mind as I opened the case, of course. I had resigned the 'apprenticeship,' and they were too simple and repetitious anyway.

Once again I played all the old things I knew so well. But this time, somehow, they didn't please me. It was as if they were played by someone else, and not too well at that. My ears were altered somehow. The image of de Luna came to me then, a memory almost, with a life of its own—his feline smile, his left hand darting effortlessly over strings and frets. But more, the music—too subtle and unfamiliar to recall distinctly.

What had he done? Was it like this? Or, was it like that? I imitated him as best I could, a very pale imitation at that, but the results were encouraging. The guitar warmed up a bit.

I opened my backpack and found the exercises don Diego had given me right on top. I unfolded them on the coffee table. They reeked of stale cigar smoke, but I paid no heed and attacked them assiduously.

I took each strum apart and carefully put it together again. I made sure I could sustain each one for 15 seconds or so without missing too many beats. And, when I'd memorized all of them, I began to experiment. For example, I tried stringing together two or more patterns into a four-bar rhythm—like this one:

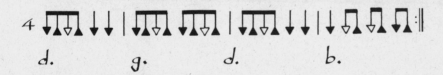

Then I tried playing chords that I knew with the rhythms, at first just one chord, then two, then one to the bar, or more . . . whatever sounded good was the rule.

I quit late in the evening, fully satisfied that I had mastered de Luna's exercises, and more than that, transformed them into creative playthings. For the second time, my guitar had lived and breathed.

All the next day I was in good spirits, anticipating the fun I was going to have playing when I got home from work. The campus was tense and it felt good to have some means of relaxation and recreation. But, strangely, the guitar was as cold as ice that evening. The flame was out. I could not produce a new idea that had any life. I could not even remember how don Diego's music had sounded. After an hour I could see the situation was not going to improve, so I set the guitar aside and fell into a mood of frustration.

Wednesday brought no improvement, and my distress worsened. Having felt this mysterious warmth twice now I didn't want to let it die—and yet there was only one sure way to rekindle the flame—the way I had rejected. As a result of the political situation and my peculiar preoccupation with the guitar, I was somewhat unresponsive in class, and slow at my homework. It began to seem that I was working against myself by *not* going back for more lessons.

By Friday night my thoughts on the matter were clear. I had resolved to return to don Diego's. I had convinced myself that I really had nothing to lose, while I stood to gain whatever came to me by way of the 'apprenticeship.' After all, I was sophisticated enough to remain aloof from don Diego's ploys. In fact, I felt morally superior about returning, for I was doing old don Diego de Luna a favor, giving him a sense of importance and self-worth. We would both be profiting.

LESSON II:

The Summit of the First Realm

i. How to Strum the Guitar—Scientifically

Reaching don Diego's door about midday Saturday, I hesitantly extended my hand to knock. But it occurred to me that a faint introduction might indicate intimidation on my part. Therefore I rapped rather boldly. The wood was unexpectedly resonant however, and I impulsively added two soft taps to cover my mistake.

"Alfonso, I thought that was you," said don Diego, answering the door. "Please, come in."

We sat down and presently, after the guitars were out, don Diego invited me to play the first exercise. I was eager to demonstrate my skill, but I was careful not to let my eagerness show. I took the exercise slowly and played it well, even adding a few extra chords for spice. Then I looked up, expecting don Diego's approval.

"Now the second," he said, taking out a cigar. There was no sign of approval or disapproval in his expression.

I finished the second in like manner, expecting now to receive the well-deserved praise.

"The third, please."

When I had finished the tenth don Diego still sat regarding me with a cool gaze. He puffed pensively at his cigar.

"Go on," he said.

"But that's all there was."

"Go on, go on—that was a good warmup—now *create* something."

I gulped. My creativity had been blocked for days. But I had no time to consider the whys and wherefores—I was not about to excuse myself and ruin my carefully cultivated image of self-confidence. I had exercised self-control until then, so I simply took a controlled plunge into improvising.

At first I struggled to find a sound in my skull, but suddenly the ideas began to flow in an unstoppable stream. The sounds I heard coming out of my guitar were better than anything I had heard at home. The clarity of my mind, the speed of my decisions startled me. It was as if something from outside had taken over my mind.

I brought the music to an end. Looking up, I encountered don Diego's face looming directly over mine. He was grinning broadly.

"Alfonso!" he exclaimed, leaning over and grabbing both my ears all of a sudden. He looked very intense and, with one eye askew, slightly deranged.

"Please, don Diego, the cigar smoke—I'll be sick."

"Alfonso!" he exclaimed, releasing my head and patting my cheek. He spun around and clapped his hands together. "You did your homework!"

"Well, yeah . . . I mean, of course."

"You did very well with it."

"Well, I . . . I worked at it."

"And more than that—you've been touched."

"I've been touched?"

"Why do you think we do exercises such as these?"

" 'Why?' "

"Yes, why do thinking human beings voluntarily sacrifice half a lifetime, hour upon precious hour, to the monotonous drudgery of practice? It is for love, that's why—it's for seduction!"

"Seduction? You mean girls?"

"To seduce the Muse—that's what I mean. And she's seen fit to flirt with you."

"She has?"

"Yes, your practice has been worthwhile. You keep at it and you'll be having an affair with her, I can almost guarantee."

"Really?"

"You're very lucky, Alfonso."

"I am? Really?"

"Yes. Now let's get on to something new."

"Then I played pretty good?"

"That's what I said."

"You liked it?"

"This cigar has gone out," said don Diego, pressing his lips together in mild disgust. He began peering about the room like a hawk. Suddenly he took his seat, produced some matches from his coat pocket and said, "Alfonso, ready your guitar. Let us get in tune, for we have a lot of ground to cover today and no time to lose."

ii. *A Quiver of Chords*

"First off I want to show you a few more chords. We'll have five when I add these, and you may know all of them already: E, A, D, G and C major? They are a very special group. Out of them come all the essential ingredients!"

"I do know those chords but I never thought of them as all that significant."

"Ah, but they are! They are! Get to know them well and the minor chords of the same name are just a step away. So are dozens, hundreds of other chords and scales, and . . ."

"Now clear up something for me, don Diego: what is the difference between a major and a minor chord?"

"For one thing, there is a difference in the emotions they touch. That's the *main* thing, Alfonso—are you listening?"

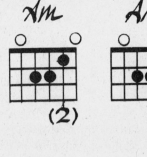

"Yes, I'm listening."

"Minor chords reach the darker feelings."

He began to strum his guitar, saying, ". . . sadness, longing, forlorn hope."

"I see."

"Major chords are typically bright and positive. Compare A major and A minor for example. Note that there is only a 'minor' change in the shadow—on string 2."

Don Diego smiled as he sketched the chord charts on his chalkboard.

"But, again, there are several possible ways to finger it."

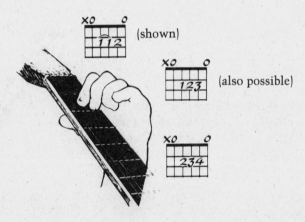

(shown)

(also possible)

"Don Diego, I notice how you can flatten your first finger over two strings. Are you double-jointed?"

"Not at all. Flexibility comes with practice."

"I know—*everything* comes with practice."

"Except *spirit*. You can't practice spirit into existence. Fortunately, we know you have it already. With practice, your spirit's wings will sprout feathers."

"Hmm."

Don Diego ripped off a colorful bar or two as if to punctuate his remark.

"Say, don Diego, since A major can be fingered in a number of ways, which way is best?"

"As I said—depends."

"Show me what you mean."

"Well, *you* tell *me*—which of these two fingerings of G major (*a* or *b*) would be best for going to the next chord, C major?" ●

"The second."

"Why?"

"Well, you can just lift up fingers 3 and 2 and put them down one set of strings over."

"Good chord chemistry, Alfonso. Now here is the last of the five basic major chords I told you about: D major. You know it, no?" Don Diego sketched as he spoke.

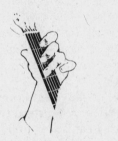

a. 210003 or

b. 320004 to ---

c. x32010

DM

D string

"Oh sure."

"Very good; can you show me three ways to pin the shadow of this chord?"

"Only two come to me right off." (*shown at right*) ●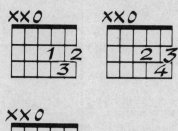

"Here is another way. Lay the first finger across three strings like this . . . and complete the chord with finger 2. (*shown at right*) ●

"This technique is called the 'bar.' "

"Oh sure, I know about barring, and bar chords."

"In D major here we have a half-bar—half the strings pinned down, and the full bar crosses all six strings . . .*"

"You know, Alfonso, you have raised a question *muy importante.*"

"Have I?"

"Yes, yes indeed—this question of the best fingering. If we don't have smoothly linked fingerings, then what have we got?—Musical hiccups."

"At the least."

"I'll tell you what I'm going to do. Before the end of today I'm going to write out some chord changes that will help you understand the art of smooth connection. But right now we had best deal with an emergency close at hand."

iii. Don Diego Meets a Threat

"What is it?" I asked apprehensively.

"It is a flaw—a crack in our system of rhythmic notation that threatens to bring the whole thing crashing down."

"Really?"

"Yes, a grave omission on my part. I forgot that besides sound there is silence. We need to notate both."

"Yes, I can see your point. What do you propose?"

"Let me meditate."

Don Diego bowed his head and held his brow with his hand.

"Yes!" he said, picking up his chalkboard and beginning to write.

"You have the solution?"

"Mm—hmm . . . first . . . I'm going to substitute a new kind of beat marker for the old one."

old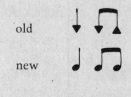

new

"A very tricky way to work up my interest—those are notes, a quarter and two eighths, I believe."

"It's no trick—these things are much better than my system! I'm only glad I remembered them. . . . Behold! There you have one bar of four–four time."

"Four–four—now what does that mean exactly?"

---

* *The bar technique is typically notated by a B for* bar, *or a C for* ceja, *and a roman numeral for the fret. Thus a full bar at the second fret would be BII or CII, less than a full bar ½BII or ½CII. A roman numeral by itself indicates the position of play for the first finger. Thus IX would mean to locate the index finger at the ninth fret from the nut, to "play at the ninth position." BIX would mean a full bar at the ninth position.*

"The top number is a carry-over from the old time signature. It means the beats are grouped in fours."

"The first of every four is accented?"

"Yes. And the four on the bottom tells you that each beat is a quarter note long. In other words, the quarter note is the unit of the beat."

"*That* I *do* not understand."

"Each beat is a unit, each unit is a quarter note."

"Sorry, I still don't get it."

"OK. As you know from foot-tapping, one beat is like any other."

"The same length of time?"

"Yes. Now we put a note value on the beat, and that is the lower number in the time signature. It is the unit of the beat."

"I see."

"It is a quarter note in 4/4, an eighth note in 4/8, it would be a sixteenth note in 4/16—but of course no one uses 4/16."

"Wait a minute—why *don't* people use 4/16 time? Is it because 16ths are too fast for most players?"

"No, no, Alfonso. Let me emphasize this point: The duration of the notes is *relative*. The *tempo* determines whether they are fast or slow. With a tempo of *adagio* this measure of 4/16 would be played quite slowly. With a tempo of *presto* it would be played quite quickly."

"Then what's the problem with 4/16 time?"

"The page would get all messy with flags and beams. You see, starting with the eighth note we add a flag or a beam to the stem each time we split the value of the note in half."

whole note

half

quarter

eighth

sixteenth

"As you can see, the split notes in 4/16 time would have three flags or beams."

"It would get messy all right."

"I think now would be a good time to slip in the matter of 'rests.' A rest means a silence—more exactly it tells you to *carry the rhythm* silently. You feel a rest just as you *feel* a note. The rests would get messy in 4/16 time, too—don't you agree?"

whole rest

half

quarter

eighth

sixteenth

"That's why we so often see the quarter note used as the unit of the beat. It's positioned conveniently between the longer and the shorter time divisions.

"To sum up then, the top number of the time signature tells you how many beats per measure. The lower number tells you what kind of note is the unit of the beat."

"How Many on top and What Kind on the bottom." *

"Yes."

"I see. But something is missing."

"Eh? What?"

"The notes only work for even-numbered divisions of time like 'Da-da, Da-da.' Well, suppose I wanted 'Di-gi-ty, Di-gi-ty, Da-da, Da-da.' "

"That would be written like this:

"Three notes on one pulse is called a triplet. We could put five, six, seven or eleven notes into a pulse too—a number written above the group would call attention to this irregular division."

How many?   Two.
What kind?   Quarter notes.

1-an-a   2-an-a   3 - &   4 - &

TYPE OF PULSE

	A	B	C
1	𝅗𝅥	𝅘𝅥	𝅘𝅥𝅮
2	𝅘𝅥 𝅘𝅥	𝅘𝅥𝅮𝅘𝅥𝅮	𝅘𝅥𝅯𝅘𝅥𝅯
3	³ 𝅘𝅥𝅘𝅥𝅘𝅥	³ 𝅘𝅥𝅮𝅘𝅥𝅮𝅘𝅥𝅮	³ 𝅘𝅥𝅯𝅘𝅥𝅯𝅘𝅥𝅯
4	𝅘𝅥𝅮𝅘𝅥𝅮𝅘𝅥𝅮𝅘𝅥𝅮	𝅘𝅥𝅯𝅘𝅥𝅯𝅘𝅥𝅯𝅘𝅥𝅯	𝅘𝅥𝅰𝅘𝅥𝅰𝅘𝅥𝅰𝅘𝅥𝅰
5	⁵	⁵	⁵

DIVISIONS OF THE PULSE

* 4/4 time is sometimes symbolized by ¢ (common meter), and 2/2 by ¢ (cut-time).

MASTERING GUITAR

"Don Diego, you kept saying 'pulse,' not *beat*."

"Yes. An example will clear up my reasons. First, here is a quarter note, one beat in 4/4 time: ♩ Now I'll subdivide it into two eighth notes, ♫ and one of the eighth notes into a triplet. ♫♪♪♪

"Now—was that eighth note we divided a beat?"

"No, the quarter note was the beat, that second eighth note was the offbeat."

"But the eighth note was a pulse in time, wasn't it?"

"Yes."

"There you have it."

"Fair enough."

"Any more questions?"

"No, I guess not."

"Then you understand everything?"

"You must be cr— . . . uh, kidding."

"You'll see, Alfonso—just trust me to show you how easily all this theory becomes practice."

"Very well—proceed."

iv. *Alfonso Fegoni—Syncopated Sight-Reader*

"Let me ask you this: Do you agree that two quarter notes equal a half note?"

"Yes, I can deduce that from your chart."

"Deduce? Let's not be fancy—it's simple musical arithmetic. Now if you can see that, you'll have no trouble playing this. But just for your reference I'll write it down in the old notation too.

"Don Diego, you told me not to let you forget . . ."

"I haven't forgotten. We're closer to syncopation than you think."

"Then let me get one question out of the way."

"Ask it, compadre."

"Suppose I wanted to extend a note for three beats in 4/4 time—now that would come to three quarter notes worth of time, right?"

"Right."

"I don't see a 'three-quarter note' anywhere on your chart."

"There, you see! You've done it."

"Done it? Done what?"

"Thrown open the door."

"The door to what?"

"Syncopation, of course. You'll see in a moment, by way of the answer to your question.

"There is a way, two ways really, to get the 'three-quarter note.' One: the dot, two: the tie.

"To dot a note is to make it one and a half times as long. Now half of a half note is a . . . ?"

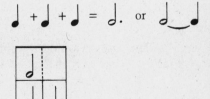

47

"A quarter note."

"So a dotted half note is a half plus . . . ?"

"A quarter."

"Which equals?"

"Three quarter notes. So it's a 'three-quarter note.'"

"In effect, but call it a *dotted half* from now on, OK? And what are these?" ●

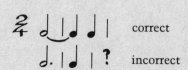

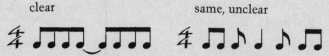

"I'll write them out," I said. ● (See answers below.)

(See answers at bottom of page.)

"Very good. Now the tie binds together the values of the notes it connects. A tie is sometimes used, as in this case, to show the middle of the bar . . .

"Here, where the note is extended over the bar line, a tie is essential."

"I see, it literally ties together the notes, as an addition sign would do."

"Correct. Now, look at the progression of ideas here":

"Syncopation."

"*Sí.* Can you figure this one?" ● (See answers below.)

v. The Slap-Twang Method

"Things have fallen into place rather suddenly, haven't they, Alfonso?"

"You do make it seem easy."

"I have but one more puzzle for you before I can give you your homework and send you on your way."

"You mean we're almost through?"

"Don't you have many responsibilities, important matters, that take up your time?"

"Well, I, uh . . . yes, of course—I am, or I will be extremely busy very soon."

"Then you wouldn't want too much guitar work to do, would you?"

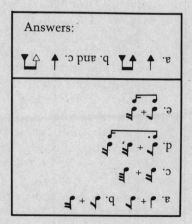

Answers:

MASTERING GUITAR

"You're right, don Diego."

I was astonished to hear so realistic an evaluation of our relationship from the imperious Diego de Luna. "This must be a change in tactics!" sounded my mental alarm. But as I looked at him writing out the next problem he seemed as meek and mild as my old chemistry prof, Dr. Wood. I shook my head and scratched behind my ear. I began to consider the notion that my fears might have been exaggerated all along—that de Luna was only dramatic, not dangerous.

"Here I have syncopated the second beat with a rest, Alfonso."

"It's rhythm number one from the ten you have been practicing. (See p. 36.) But how would you stop a chord so suddenly and for so short a time as an eighth note rest?"

"Well, here we are, back to the palm slap at last."

"Oh yeah, the palm slap could do that, I guess."

"Here, first practice going 'slap-twang-slap-twang' over and over —like this: ●

"Good. Now try this, a stroke on one beat followed by a 'slap-twang' on the next beat. ●

"Why don't you try doing rhythm No. 1 now?"

"Looks easier than what I was just doing." ●

"Ah, Alfonso, it pleases me to see how well you can play this, but the rest of the ten may not be so easy, so let me give you a few hints."

"Let me guess. Go as slow as possible at first, so slow it almost falls apart."

"Yes, that will give you time to coordinate the palm slap."

"And you want me to set the tempo with a bar of straight quarter notes leading into the exercise?"

"Yes. Count '1, 2, 3, 4' and then begin."

"That's all I can think of."

"There is one more. When you have a tough rhythm, pretend the beat is on the eighth note."

"Eight–eight time?"

"Yes, eight eighth notes to the bar, each one getting a beat. Then you can get a true feel for where the rests fall.

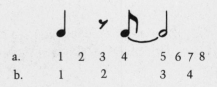

a.   1 2 3 4   5 6 7 8
b.   1   2   3   4

"When you can play it fast and fluid in 8/8, resume 4/4 (two eighth notes to the beat instead of one) and it is done.

"And so are we, Alfonso, just as I promised."

vi. *Perspective from the First Peak*

Don Diego insisted I have some wine while he wrote out the homework, and though I made a polite refusal I actually welcomed the opportunity to talk to him on a more informal basis.

Don Diego was a long time writing and before I knew it I had drunk two glasses—very potent at that altitude—hence I became a bit bold.

"Don Diego?"

"Yes?"

"What was the purpose of . . . well of . . . the first time we met, that is . . ."

"I'm glad you brought that up. I did get excited as I recall—perhaps I owe you an apology—but I certainly didn't mean to frighten you off. I hadn't eaten in some time, you see, and it does things to a man's mind."

"Of course," I said, not totally convinced I was hearing the truth, ". . . and now that we've had a chance to, well—get acquainted, I see you are not as, as . . ."

"Oh go ahead, Fegoni, untie your tongue—I'm not as moonstruck, as crazy, as you thought—isn't that what you were about to say?"

Don Diego leaned forward, gesturing. Though he was grinning, I was afraid his excitement might at any moment turn to anger.

"That's putting it rather strongly, don Diego."

"You know, it was just fate I was named 'de Luna.' So I happen to be a bit eccentric—that has nothing to do with it. But you must suspect that if de Luna is not so crazy as at first he seemed, then perhaps he plays games with you, eh? I can see it in your face."

He sipped and smacked his lips. I hesitated to answer. Swirling the wine, he looked into the glass.

"Well, Alfonso, what if . . ."

"Don Diego, really—I didn't mean to get off onto this subject . . ."

". . . what if you are right?"

". . . and I . . . I'm right?"

"Yes. What if I were to admit to you that I am a little more than just a guitar teacher?"

"What are you then?"

"What if I were to admit I was actually the agent of a foreign power . . . and my purpose is just to disrupt your work at the University?" He continued contemplating the glass and smiling.

"Is that really what you are?" I asked, trying to evade expressing an opinion.

"Listen, Alfonso," he frowned, "disregard what I said. It was a poor joke. Maybe I'm a little uncomfortable with my humble status as compared to you—a man of science, a representative of a large and powerful country."

Don Diego suddenly seemed much more human to me.

"Yes, a poor joke, and I apologize." He looked contrite.

"That's all right, don Diego."

"If you think I'm getting bats in my belfry with my old age, you're entitled to such an opinion."

"No, I don't think that."

"Oh, of course you do," he said, then suddenly brightening up: "Come on now, let me show you this homework." He began to shuffle the papers.

"Wait, can we get back to my original question?"

"What question?"

"I don't really understand certain, uh, aspects of our first lesson."

"If you think back, perhaps you can tell me what the purpose of our first lesson was."

"You mean I should know?"

"You said it yourself."

"What?"

"The First Principle. Because of your insight I found you a suitable apprentice."

"The First Principle?"

"Didn't you say, in essence, 'One cannot cook if one does not know the ingredients?' "

"I said something like that, yes. But I . . ."

"Alfonso, you have already made tremendous progress in knowing the ingredients."

"Really?"

"Oh yes. When you played for me the very first time, you were blind to the dynamic possibilities of your guitar. Now you are not. This has increased the freedom and the expressive power of your spirit.

"Secondly, you are developing control of time. Before, it was like watching a young man dance with a beautiful woman and, like a puppy dog, he trips her up and does not even seem to notice."

I was openly amused at this image of myself. Now I was beginning to understand the meaning of don Diego's dramatics.

"There you are, Alfonso! You're loosening up a bit, too. That is good! I will drink to that. Relaxing has a hell of a lot to do with your progress."

"Must be those syncopated rhythms."

"Ha! That will do it every time. Have another glass of wine. Now, point three, my friend, is that you are beginning to read music, and—though reading is not an 'ingredient' in itself—I would venture to say it is an indispensable ability to the good cook."

"What are the 'ingredients' you keep speaking of, don Diego?"

"The ingredients add up to physical control of the sound-making capabilities of the guitar. You must know *what* these capabilities are and *how* to make them manifest.

"Look at it this way—give some bananas and a few spices to Alfonso Fegoni and he will, after several hours in the kitchen, produce a respectable, edible banana mush. But give the same ingredients to a cook of any merit and he will, in ten minutes, create a dish. And that dish, Alfonso, though made from humble bananas and little else, will be an experience!"

"I begin to see now. You're saying even a simple piece done with control of the expressive elements can sound good."

". . . Better! *Better* than a difficult piece done mushily. But young guitarists are inclined to race ahead, thinking they are getting better by playing more and more advanced pieces . . ."

"But that's not so."

"No, of course not. So, to sum up: developing impeccable control over your instrument's voice—this is the first stage of your apprenticeship."

"What is the next stage?"

"The first is quite enough for now."

"Why can't you tell me?"

"It would be harmful."

"Why? How do you know?"

"There is enough in front of you right now—any more and it would be risking everything."

"Risking . . . *everything!*"

"Yes, haven't you gathered by now that this is a serious business you're into?"

Don Diego chuckled and gulped down the last of his wine. My pride was hurt and I was confused once again. Why hadn't don Diego just told me about "The First Principle" when first we met? Had he or had he not meant to frighten me? Why was he hiding things from me? "Risking everything?" What did he mean by that?

vii. Don Diego Takes Alfonso Through Some Changes

"Come on, Alfonso, let us look at this homework.

"This is the first part—the chord changes that show how to connect chords smoothly.

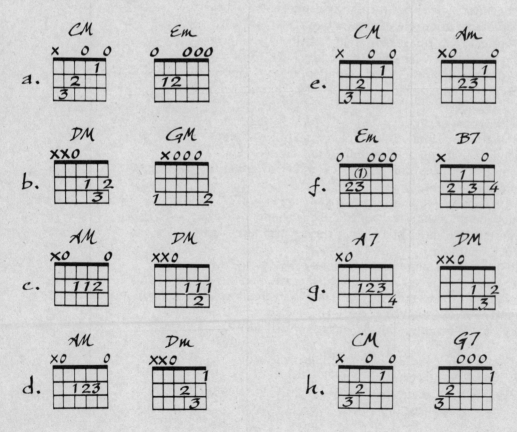

"(a), C major to E minor, shows the use of a 'pivot finger.' When-ever you can do so comfortably you should carry over a finger from one chord to the next. See how I do it here: One—

"Two—

"Three."

One

Two

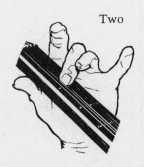

Three

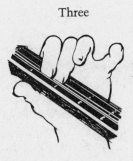

"Simple enough."

"In (b)—D major to G major—the middle finger slides along string one. This is an example of a 'guide finger.' "

"Guide fingers and pivot fingers help to keep you from losing your place, right?"

"Right. Notice how, in G major, the index finger has to lean over and touch string 5." (*shown at right*)

"Is that wrong?"

"It's right! The finger is damping the string."

"Because string 5 shouldn't sound?"

"It's not part of the chord. Now in (f) we have a beautiful tech-nique for smoothing connections—the 'prepared note.' While you're playing E minor you put the index finger behind the ring finger on string 4. Then there's no time spent searching for the note on the fourth string when you change to B dominant 7."

"E minor just *dissolves* into B7!"

"Like butter into hot toast, Alfonso."

"I was thinking more of NaCl into H_2O, don Diego."

"What's the formula for good wine, Alfonso? I want you to conjure me up a bit more of this vintage."

"It would be difficult. I couldn't make much more than fifty or sixty gallons at a time."

"*Caramba!* Alfonso, could you really?"

"I might consider doing it—if . . ."

"If what?"

"If you explain the dominant seventh chord to me."

"Cheap price."

"Cheap wine."

Don Diego frowned.

"No, not really, don Diego—I want something else, too."

"Ah! Here's the fine print you gringos are so famous for."

"I want a foretaste, a preview of the next lesson."

"Oh no, no, no . . . it's out of the question."

"Why so?"

"Do you think that just because I've had a little to drink, I would be so careless as to reveal the Second Realm of Guitar Knowledge to you?"

"The Second Realm of Guitar Knowledge? What is that?"

Don Diego brought the wine glass to his lips. "Alfonso, let's drop the subject right there."

He sounded very final, but I had to press him further. "Is that the same as the next 'stage' of the apprenticeship?"

"No, Alfonso, it is not—it is the Second Realm—now that is all I can say."

"You've never mentioned this before, don Diego. Can you tell me just . . ."

"No! I can't discuss it."

"OK, OK."

"Now the dominant seventh chord is another matter. I will gladly explain that. The dominant seventh chord is a major chord with one distinctive note added to it. This one note changes the nature of the chord entirely."

"Can you show it to my ears, don Diego?"

"Of course. Here is an E major chord, and here, one note added, is E dominant 7.

"It is full of tension and expectancy. All this tension is released when one changes to A major . . . ahhh, you see?"

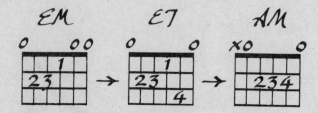

"I see! I *hear*, that is."

"I could say more, but let me go on to explain the rest of the homework.

"These rhythms are the same as the ten you memorized last week, only redone with rests, or dots, and ties. Your problem is to match the old rhythms with the new ones. For example, we know how arrow-rhythm (a) looks already, and here it is in the new notation, the fourth one down. You just write an (a) next to the 4. Number 8 is also rhythm (a), but done with a dot, rather than a rest. The remainder of them you must decipher yourself.

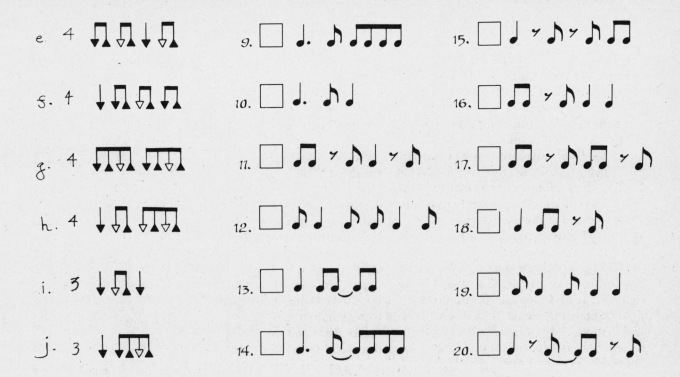

"After you have learned to read and play all the rhythms, play the chord progressions to them to test your coordination. Then you can try playing these chord progressions—any rhythm you like.

a.

Am |EM |Am |EM |A7 |Dm |Am EM* |Am :|■

b.

DM |GM |A7 |DM |B7 |Em |A7 |DM :|■

c.

GM |Em |CM |DM |GM |Am |DM |B7 |

Em |Am |Em |CM |GM |Am |DM |GM |■

d.

AM-DM |EM |AM-DM |EM |AM-DM |Dm |

AM-EM |AM :|■

e.

CM |GM-G7 |CM |GM-G7 |

Am-EM |Am-Dm |CM-G7 |CM :|■

f.

CM |G7 |CM |G7 |CM |Am |⌐1.⌐ Dm |G7 :||

⌐2.⌐
Dm-G7 |CM :|■

* When two chords appear in a single measure, use your intuition to find the "right" spot to change. The usual practice is to give half the measure to each chord. For example, bars 7 and 8 of (a) might be done:

Bars 1 and 2 of (d):

Answers.

1.h 2.c 3.f 4.a 5.f
6.i 7.e 8.a 9.c 10.i
11.e 12.g 13.i 14.b
15.b 16.d 17.g 18.i
19.d 20.h

viii. Alfonso's Gambit

Don Diego settled back in his chair and pulled out yet another cigar. I could tell by the way he fumbled for a light, the sound of his voice, and his good humor that he was drunk. Perhaps now, I thought, he would be more open to discussing this 'Second Realm of Guitar Knowledge' *if* I employed a measure of subtlety, that is.

"Are there only two realms of guitar knowledge, don Diego?"

"Two? Two?" he giggled. "No. There are three. There are three . . . like three mountain peaks to climb."

"Three? What does mastery of these three mean, don Diego?"

"The end of the first stage of one's apprenticeship in the art."

"Oh, I see—then all three have to do with developing more control over . . ."

Don Diego interrupted.

"This wine has made my brain very sluggish, Alfonso. How delightfully it prolongs the afternoon! Would you like some more?"

"A little bit, please. Thank you. As you were about to say?"

"Ah yes. My mind is soaked in the grape, but still not too spongy to see you are trying to trick me into telling you more about the Second Realm of Guitar Knowledge. And though your persistence is to your credit, any more discussion is, as I have said, out of the question. A toast to your persistence?"

"Well, don Diego, I guess you're too much for me to match wits with. May I ask you another question—on what we've covered already that is?"

"Be my guest."

"You've said the first stage of apprenticeship is to develop impeccable control over the guitar's sound-making capabilities, right?"

"You listened well. But don't leave out 'expressiveness.' After all, what is all this sound-making capability for? The feelings . . . the feelings are the most . . ."

"Just how difficult a task is that?"

"Eh?"

"How difficult is it to pass through the first stage?"

"Oh," he said wistfully, "it's never really over. That's how difficult it is."

"Oh, then even you haven't accomplished perfection in this yet?"

"No, no-ho-ho, heavens no!" Then he suddenly sharpened his expression. "But I allow my guitar to *think* I have. Ai—I should watch my tongue, she probably heard me." Evidently switching to a thought of his gardening he added, "But I must trim and rake and water constantly or the weeds begin to grow."

"The weeds?"

"Yes, my age is the reason. My technique is not as strong as it once was. Fortunately, I've learned the strength there is in utter relaxation. It's been quite a struggle," he chuckled, "trying to get the most response with the least energy. The older I get, the more I must relax. Someday I will play the guitar without touching it."

He slurped at his glass and sighed in satisfaction.

"Ahh . . . you see, tension betrays the slowness of an older man's nerves. But when the *mind* rises above the piece—there is no inefficiency, and I play faster than you twenty-year-olds."

"What do you mean by 'the mind rising above the piece'?"

"When I relax," he said, blinking in pleasure at his subject, "I stay serene above the entire plan of the music. I can look over it from one end to the other—like an eagle, you see? My hands, making their way through the thicket of movements down below, are informed of all that is happening for miles ahead. They move only when they must, just how they must—there is no inefficiency!"

"So it's a struggle just to make it easy."

"That's why the sky isn't cluttered with eagles, amigo. Didn't I say this is a serious undertaking? It requires all of your resources, and some you never knew you had."

"Hmm, don Diego. What a challenge this first task is. Complex, demanding—why it's probably almost as rough as calculus."

Don Diego narrowed his eyes. "Calculus? What is that?"

"You've never heard of it?"

"I think once, but it was a long time ago. I've forgotten."

"Well, let me tell you. It is a truly awesome obstacle that's routinely placed in the paths of science undergraduates."

"You don't say . . . difficult is it?"

"Oh yes, *very.*"

"Tell me more about it."

"Well, lots of students can't stand it. Their minds degenerate into total confusion—often after only a matter of a few days' exposure."

Don Diego leaned forward in his seat, fascinated, by the look of him. "Nooo," he said in wonderment.

"Oh yes. They drop like flies the first of every quarter. It's a pathetic spectacle. When you walk through the dormitories you often hear cries of desperation and mental anguish."

"And it's the calculus behind all that?"

"Oh yeah, nine times out of ten."

"Incredible! How long does it take to master this calculus? Er, what is it anyway?"

"Oh, it's a system for adding infinities of little bits of nothingness."

"What a beautiful thing."

"And it takes about two years of constant effort to become competent with it."

"Yes—well, how many can pass the course? Two, three out of the school?"

"No, no . . . at least fifty percent get through eventually."

Don Diego leaned back in his chair, grinning through his cigar.

"Well, it must be difficult, difficult indeed—but not as difficult as the first task of the apprentice guitarist."

"Gee, most calculus students wouldn't think so, I'd bet on that."

"How would you know, Alfonso Puppy Dog?"

"Oh, shoot, I don't really know, not having heard all there is to hear about the first task—this new realm of guitar knowledge, for example—so, you're right, I can't really say . . . and I'm sure it *is* very difficult—still, I can hardly believe it would be more difficult than calculus."

"Why not, Alfonso? I want you to speak your mind! You are hedging!"

He was growing noticeably irritated, and so, proceeding cautiously, I capitalized on this.

"Well, OK, don Diego, but please remember, if I say something that seems impertinent, that it's only because of my ignorance, and that you asked me . . ."

"Yes, yes, of course—now get on with it."

"Well, here you are, don Diego—you're going to show me this second step, or whatever, in our next lesson, and, as you have said, there are only three steps . . ."

"Peaks, Alfonso—peaks! Three noble summits to conquer!"

"Right, right—peaks. And, anyway, that's two out of three in such short order. It's all going by so fast, it seems, well . . . it seems like it can't be more than a trick or two, and after that, a matter of keeping in trim, as you say."

"Now you listen here, my impudent friend!" said don Diego, coming to his feet a bit unsteadily, "I'll tell you what's a trick and what isn't! Your calculus is no more than a bag of tricks! It is merely a mental sleight of hand—that's what it is! Very impressive, I'm sure, but the Second and the Third Realms are matters of the spirit—they are not sleight of hand, as you seem to think! They are approached with the totality of one's self! You have no idea what that means, do you?"

"Uh, no . . . no, I have no idea, none at all."

"Then hand me that guitar! I'll show you what it means! Come on, pass it over, pass it over!"

I quickly handed him the guitar. Full of furious intensity, he sat down and, without hesitation, began driving the bass strings with his thumb. It was a relentless 4/4 beat, and only the herald of what was to come—which was the incredible Second Realm of Guitar Knowledge.

PART TWO
●
THE SECOND REALM
OF GUITAR KNOWLEDGE

Dropping Out of the Second Realm

i. The Forzosa Effect

"Serenading someone this evening, Mr. Fegoni?"

Serenading! A typical example of Dr. Forzosa's snide humor. I braced my arms against the steering wheel, took a deep breath and, exhaling, sagged back into the car seat. That really clinched it, I was going to have to keep my guitar and the school out of sight of each other from now on. I looked out the car window at the passing scenery. It was a sunny Saturday morning and I was driving west out of Caracas toward don Diego's town and my third encounter with the mercurial guitar teacher.

My meeting with Forzosa had been only the day before. He'd been cordial enough, really, and the same remark from a fellow student would probably have amused me, but coming as it did from Dr. Felix Forzosa, head of the graduate department, School of Chemical Engineering, University of Caracas, Venezuela, there were certain uncomfortable connotations.

But I have scarcely said a word in description of this most prominent figure about the campus. It was Forzosa, of course, who had called me the morning of the riots, and who had become irritated as he found out that I had merely overslept our appointment and knew nothing about the brewing trouble on the campus. Now, two weeks later, I had a much richer appreciation of this man.

It is easiest to begin sketching Forzosa by comparing him to de Luna. They were opposites in many ways, physically and mentally.

De Luna was slightly taller than me (I am five eight and a half). He was skinny, wiry, energetic, and quick, with extreme variety in his voice, gestures, and facial expressions.

Forzosa was around fifty years old, a bullish little man, compact, solid, restrained and deliberate in his movements. He was highly self-controlled, but in his manner of walking he showed the aggressiveness that made him well suited for the role of an administrator. He marched along swiftly in hurried little steps, scarcely looking left or right on his way through the throngs of students. They melted around him.

This aggressiveness was also visible in Forzosa's eyes. They were nervous—probing, testing, evaluating—although he could at the same time be talking in his characteristically slow, precise and even voice. Being extremely nearsighted, he was never without a pair of thick, black-framed glasses that made his small, square-cornered eyes look even smaller. There was a warmth to de Luna's eyes, permanently etched in his wrinkles; Forzosa's eyes were cool, and cut like a pair of surgical tools.

Forzosa favored dark-toned, three-piece suits, and white shirts with starched collars that cut slightly into the fat on his neck. Black and white clothing is popular in Venezuela, and this may explain his taste to some degree, but not his stiff formality. During lectures he'd grip his open lapels, or hook a thumb in a vest pocket, then he'd nod left and right from the waist, declaiming in a lackluster voice, while the gold medal hanging from his watch chain flipped back and forth, flashing. He did not know how to talk without sounding as though he was reading from a book.

Except for his meticulously trimmed moustache, he generally looked as if he had just scraped his face clean with a straight razor. The moustache extended precisely to the borders of his mirthless mouth like a strip of salt and pepper tape. He had a prominent chin, fleshy jowls, and his dome was nearly free of hair. On the sides, the hair was closely cropped.

To complete the picture, he smoked a stubby, handsome briar pipe that he could never keep lit for very long.

Forzosa had a hand on the pulse of the University—that is to say, he had a lot to do with obtaining and channeling the considerable sums funneled into the chemical engineering department by Venezuelan oil companies. This endeared him to the higher administration. He was very secure.

However, he was not particularly popular with students, and they were not popular with him. Saying that he "disliked students" to a class full of undergraduates was a joke he never tired of. But he did his job extremely well. This was due to his phenomenal memory and attention to detail. He was uninventive, but had a thorough and precise command of facts. Through overpreciseness he frequently got into arguments. His bullheadedness occasionally would send an opponent stomping out of the room, something Forzosa actually seemed to relish. He'd grin and make a snide remark. The man's humor had a nasty edge whenever possible.

There was one splash of color in the life of Dr. Felix Forzosa. It was the large, pastel collection of Latin American butterflies he kept in velvet-lined glass cases on the walls of his office.

I had tried to avoid Forzosa ever since the first time I had met him. But unfortunately I had two classes with him. This complicated matters considerably.

"Do you have anything to add to the opinion of Mr. Delgado, Mr. Fegoni?"

"No," I answered in general. The thoughts I had tried to voice in class had for some reason come out haltingly or wrong. I was making a poor impression. The first week, when I'd been distracted by the riots and preoccupied with the guitar, had set the tempo.

This gives some of the background against which I measured Forzosa's remark. I wanted to keep a low profile, yet now he undoubtedly had me tagged as the guitarist of his department. How could he take me seriously, considering my behavior in class and my constantly and conspicuously dragging a guitar about?

"Absolutely no guitar at school," I resolved again as I looked out the window, "even if it does cut my practice time to the bone."

At the moment of this internal argument I was passing through an extensive and ugly industrial district. The drab landscape had a depressing effect on me. The ranks of box-like buildings and roads fanned by like the dusty cliffs and arroyos of a mechanized desert. Railroad cars, trucks, and tanker rigs moved about like grazing dinosaurs in this nonhuman landscape.

"Maybe it would be wisest to quit de Luna right now, quit him altogether," I thought. The glimpse of the Second Realm I had stolen through trickery the previous week had been intriguing, but how could I keep up with the guitar work when my school work was pickling? How could I dare risk such a juggling act? The dilemma was upon me again, and again I felt forced to the same conclusion.

"I shall quit, and I shall tell de Luna today," I decided. "It wouldn't be right not to tell him. He may be off his rocker a bit, but he deserves to be treated with respect. It will hurt his feelings, but it would be worse if I just dropped out of sight. I'll simply explain that I can't live up to what he requires of a pupil."

I was satisfied with that and, feeling better, glanced sideways. Rural countryside was replacing the factories and freightyards. Soon I'd turn onto the mountain road that led up to don Diego's town.

As I relaxed, my mind returned to the moment when de Luna had seized the guitar a week earlier, when his nimble fingers had begun to conjure up what had seemed to me then like a shimmering palace of notes in the air. But he'd scarcely gotten started when he slapped the strings into silence with his right hand. Then he'd got to his feet and begun to pace the floor, saying he'd never made such a stupid mistake before. Impatiently he'd asked me what time it was, claimed he had a pressing appointment, and shooed me out the door.

But don Diego had given away what the Second Realm was all about; it was fingerpicking, basically—that is, chords in the left hand, picking the strings with the right hand. He had played it with all his inimitable flair, but as I thought about what I'd heard, I realized it was fingerpicking, and that's all. During the week, the glitter had worn off the memory. It made quitting that much easier.

I looked over at the bottle of wine on the car seat. The promise had been for 60 gallons, and this was not even one sixtieth that much. But I felt I should repair the dent I'd made in his supply. He would gladly have let me drink the last drop in the house, I was sure. I had been thinking this bottle might bring out some more answers to certain mysteries about de Luna. Now it could serve another purpose, it could cushion the blow of my giving up the apprenticeship.

The road passed into the shadows of a canyon and began to wind its way upward. In an hour or so it would deliver me out into the highland valley where don Diego's town was situated. There was a sense of anticipation—the view unfolds suddenly as you round a curve. The shadowy canyon cliffs part like the blades of a pair of shears, revealing a landscape bathed in sunlight. Still at a distance, you see the bare white walls of the town clustered under the steep green mountains, like a flock of gulls that have come inland to escape a storm.

ii. The Bridge Between Two Realms

As I walked up the path to don Diego's I had a growing sense of discomfort about the situation. How, exactly, was I going to word my resignation? How was I going to let him down easy? But then I began to think my apprehensions were exaggerated. Well, either way, the thing to be avoided was indecisiveness.

At last I reached the door and knocked. The latch turned and it swung open.

"Well, Alfonso, you're early."

"Hello, don Diego."

"Come in, come in." Smiling, he stood back and gestured with an open hand.

As soon as I put down the guitar I yanked the bottle out of the sack.

"Ah! What is this? Wine? You brought this for me?"

"I'm sorry I couldn't distill the 60 gallons I promised, but I think I've made up for quantity with quality."

"This pleases me very much, amigo, I am very grateful. But you did not have to do this, I really expected nothing, nothing at all. Uh, by the way, is that cheese and crackers you've got there?"

"Yes, fruit, too . . . here."

"Thank you."

"You're welcome. You know this is the least I could do, since you don't ask anything in return for the lessons."

"I get by, Alfonso. I do not like to mix the teaching of guitar and money."

"The dealer told me it was an exceptional wine, don Diego. I'm anxious to see what you think of it."

"Yes, I can see it's something special—just look at this fancy label. This is not the kind of wine one drinks just to pass the time. I will save it for a special occasion."

"Well, don Diego, in a way today *is* a special occasion."

"No, I think I will reserve it for the day you have finally traversed the Three Realms of Guitar Knowledge," he said, obliviously contemplating the bottle.

It took him a moment to store the wine in his cramped little kitchen. He came back munching on crackers and cheese, with an elfish smile on his face.

"We'll celebrate when that day comes, Alfonso—I'll take you into town and you can join me and my friends at the bar where we play our music. Playing in front of an audience—that's where you can really learn. Say, you look a little under the weather or something, amigo. Do you feel sick?"

"No."

"Something troubling you?"

"Well, yes. You see, it's a combination of too much school work and . . ."

"Wait, say no more! You are not as worn out as you think, it's that filthy air down in Caracas. You've got to stretch your lungs, refresh your blood! Here, let's take some deep breaths."

"Well, I . . . I"

"Come on, Alfonso, breathe in, breathe out, one, two, three, four!"
Reluctantly I went along in the motions.

"Don Diego . . ."

"One, two . . ."

"Don Diego! I don't think this is going to help."

"What? No? What's wrong, then?"

"Well, ever since last week I've been thinking."

"Don't tell me, I know."

"You know what?"

"You feel like quitting, right?"

"Yes, yes, I'm afraid so," I said with relief, surprised that he'd said it for me.

"That's too bad, too bad. I knew it, though—I knew a glimpse of the Second Realm could tip the balance."

"I don't think that has a lot to do with it."

"But it does—traversing the Three Realms is like walking a narrow trail along a precipice. If you look over the side into the awesome depth of it, it can unnerve you, and you are left clinging to one spot in fear, or you may fall right in. You need a guide to point out a step at a time. If you only need to worry about a step at a time, you can make it. You risk everything by looking ahead too far."

"Is that what you meant last week when you said 'risking everything,' merely that I'd quit? I'm not quitting the guitar, you know, I'm just saying I can't come up here every week. And I can't give your teaching the concentrated study it deserves."

"Alfonso, what do you understand about the Three Realms of Guitar Knowledge? There is more at stake here than a few circus tricks on the strings and frets. If you quit now you may forfeit your only chance to bring a unique expression of your spirit out into the world —that's what's at stake."

"Oh, I see, I see."

"No, Alfonso, I can tell by your voice that you do not see. Besides, if you saw, you could not be forced to quit, not for one million dollars. But it's my fault, I got drunk, I showed you the Second Realm. I bear the responsibility for this turn of events."

"Now, don Diego, do you think that's fair? I mean . . ."

"Listen, Alfonso," he said, brightening up with an idea, "maybe if I showed you how *simple* the Second Realm of Guitar Knowledge really is, then you wouldn't feel like quitting, eh?"

I thought for a second. On the one side of me I heard don Diego's rippling guitar music, on the other side I seemed to hear Professor Forzosa saying, "Serenading someone this evening, Mr. Fegoni?" But Forzosa was coming from all the way back in Caracas.

"I guess I'd hate to think that I came all this way just to turn around and go back home. So, please, show me how simple it is. It probably won't influence me to change my mind one way or the other, but I'd like to know what it's all about."

"Would you believe it is so simple that I can hand you the whole secret in *one* sentence? One sentence that will switch on light bulbs in your brain?"

"All right, let's hear it," I said skeptically.

"*Not* so fast. I want to be sure you appreciate what I'm going to tell you. I have the feeling you think you already know a little about the Second Realm."

"What makes you think that?"

"It's just a good guess, knowing Alfonso Fegoni. But what about it? Care to try to explain the Second Realm to me in your own terms? I'm waiting."

"Well, uh, . . . it's fingerpicking. That's the way I see it."

"Huh?"

"Fingerpicking. *You* know . . ."

"Fingerpicking, fingerpicking—what the hell is this fingerpicking?"

"Well, it's this," I said, starting to feel pressured. I uncased my guitar, put it on my knee and began to pluck out a folk song accompaniment I knew. The guitar was out of tune. Don Diego nodded, turning the corners of his mouth down and pushing his lip up. I stopped and looked at him in exasperation.

"You still haven't put it into words I can understand," he said.

"Well, I . . ." I started to say, becoming very heated. Don Diego leaned forward suddenly and raised his index finger.

"In one sentence, Alfonso, this is the principle: in the First Realm we strummed *six* strings, in the Second Realm we strum *selected* strings—*selected* strings, Alfonso!"

Before I could reply he grabbed his guitar.

"Look here, Alfonso, what did you do in the First Realm, eh? Down and up, down and up; thumb and finger, thumb and finger; one–and, two–and, three–and, four–and, right, eh? Right?"

"Yes, yes, yes."

"OK, you've got your guitar right there, do it on just one string, do it on the third string. Pluck it with the thumb and index finger, down and up, down and up, and count vigorously: One–and, two–and, three–and, four–and . . ."

Curious as to what could possibly be so profound about this, I picked away at the third string and counted aloud.

"Count *vigorously*, Alfonso, I can't hear whether you're playing in four–four, or *eighty*–four time." ●

Don Diego looked intently at my hand.

"Let's clear up some mechanical details, amigo. You have three weak spots in your technique, here, here, and here."

Don Diego indicated the three points on my hand marked A, B, and C.

"In the first place, bracing the little finger against the soundboard to get leverage on the strings will keep you from maneuvering over all the strings with all the fingers, as eventually you must. It keeps you from having a concise, uniform stroke, too."

"But having a brace is helpful, isn't it? Besides leverage it keeps you in touch with where you are on the guitar, doesn't it?"

"I agree, I agree. Have you ever thought of bracing your hand on the strings themselves as an alternative?"

"Let's see, like this? Planting my middle finger on string 2 and ring finger on string 1?"

"Yes, and letting your little finger dangle. Try playing string 3 with the thumb and index finger *now*," he said with an air of triumph. ●

"But that only works some of the time," I argued.

"One finger or another is usually available. Sometimes you can plant the thumb on one of the strings while the fingers play. You dance

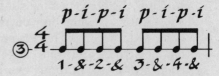

p = thumb. (from *pulgar* in Spanish)
i = index finger. (*indice* in Spanish)
3 = string 3 - see Appendix A

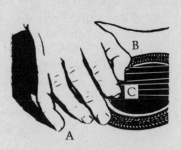

from one support to another. But you can learn to get along with no support at all, just as well. You discover how to balance the forces through trial and error."

"What's the second point about my technique?"

"Your thumb is curling, or worming, every time you make a stroke. Yet is is possible to get a better sound with much less motion. Here is how: first, you hold the thumb out to the side, so that the thumbtip is parallel to the strings.

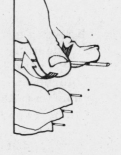

"Good, now find the contact point with the string. It is just under the left corner of the nail.

"Now pluck the string with a concise, semicircular stroke.

"By using the flesh under the corner of the nail you get the same rich sound you did previously while strumming, only now it is on selective strings, you see?"

"I'm beginning to see, don Diego," I said, and in a kind of non-verbal answer I improvised something like that depicted below with the rhythm superimposed on a chart of the strings.

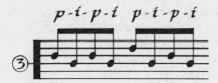

"You have the right idea, Alfonso. From the basic motion on the third string, widen the path of the thumbstroke to strings 4, 5, and 6. ●

"The third point I wanted to make has to do with the course of the fingerstrokes.

"You tend to play with the thumb and finger opposite each other, like this (*1 at right and C on page 66*), when it is better for them to pass by one another like so (*2 at right*). Then they are not stopping each other from making their full power.

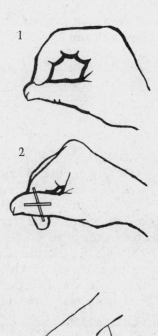

"Notice the 'X' made by the thumb crossing over the index finger. Your current habit will be much easier to break if you think about preserving the X while you play. You should be able to see it at any time you look down at your right hand.

"To find out how proper finger action should *feel*, play the third string as you did before, but making sure there is at least one inch between the points where the thumb and index finger contact the string. ●

"Good, Alfonso, very good."

"You can pick really fast with this method, can't you, don Diego?"

"*Dedillo* (pronounced de-DEE-yo) is the proper name for this technique, and yes, Alfonso, it is fast—excellent for scales and melodies."

iii. Elementary Note Knowledge

"Can we change strings? I'm getting tired of this one."

"Which one?" asked don Diego.

"Number three, of course."

"Name?"

"Name, name, name . . . I forget, wait, it's G."

"Right! To show you some other things about the Second Realm I will need to employ the five-line staff. I feel you are more than ready for this step, and besides, you want a break from noodling on that everlasting G string."

Don Diego got some music paper from the cabinet where he kept his cigars.

"I warn you, Alfonso, this subject matter is terribly difficult to understand. It takes a normal mind years to learn how the lines and spaces relate to the strings and frets. However, since I am dealing with you, rather than a normal mind, I think I can convey everything in, say, about six minutes."

"One minute for each string, eh?"

"Very astute. Now, the third string is the second line—easy enough?"

"What exactly is that curlicue sign on the left?"

"A *clef*, specifically, the G-clef, sometimes called the treble or violin clef, too. There are other clefs, but since they aren't used in guitar music, we'll leave them aside. You'll notice that this one circles and crosses the second line, certifying it as G and no other note.

"Now, I'm sure you remember that E, A, and D are the names of strings 6, 5, and 4? Well, here is how they look on the staff.

"Now . . ."

"Wait a minute! What are those short little lines?"

"*Ledger lines*—they add extra spaces and lines for extra notes."

"Maybe this sounds like a dumb question, but is there any difference between the notes represented by the spaces and the notes represented by the lines?"

"None in particular. These are the names of the spaces, and these are the lines [(a) and (b) below], and as you can see, there's an F in the first space, and an F on the top line, too.

"Put the spaces and the lines together and you get an alphabet that goes up to G and then starts over again on A. There are only seven letter names for notes, and they repeat themselves as if on a continuous loop.

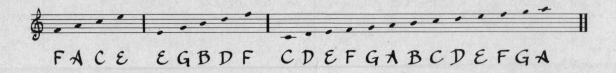

"But don Diego, *surely* you don't expect me to memorize all this?"

"Indeed not."

"You don't?"

"That's what I said. I just wanted you to see how the staff works. We can get by famously on just six notes, the notes for the open strings."

"That's good, I can handle that, I think, *maybe.*"

"You've practically done it already—just add two more, B and E."

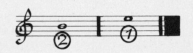

"Now Alfonso, a quick quiz: Which string is this? And this? And this one? And these two? How about these three?" ●

iv. Cornerstone of the Second Realm

"My friend, we've reached a turning point in the discussion, so I want to remind you briefly of what we've just covered. It seems like a lot, but it is very simple at the root.

"First, you've learned to pluck separate strings just by refining the strumming motion you already know so well. Second, you've begun to strengthen your technique by learning how to move your right hand, particularly to preserve an X between the thumb and index finger. And third, you've learned to recognize the notes belonging to the six strings. Have I cut it down to the bare bones for you?"

"So far so good."

"Let's see how good you are at imitation. Can you do this? You see, I am picking the D string with my thumb and then the G string with my index finger in slow eighth notes."

"Ridiculously simple."

"Not so ridiculous—keep the X."

"Oh, ahem, slipped a little."

"Here's how I'd write that out, amigo:

"The stems of thumbstroke notes generally point down, to make them stand apart from the fingerstroke notes. Now, the thumbstroke is coming on the beat, on the quarter note, in other words, so I make all the thumbstroke notes quarter notes, and join them into the overall rhythm, which is in eighth notes. Can you read this? Do watch the X, please. ●

"Good, and this?" ●

Don Diego seemed to be making sure, in his usual manner, that I could play an exercise for around 15 seconds or so without making a mistake, no matter how easy it looked.

"Sometimes we pinch two strings or more at once, too, Alfonso. This is the easiest time to forget the X between the thumb and index finger, but I can provide you with a model of the finger action that will help you get it right. Think of the right edge of your chair as the spar on the center spindle of a roulette wheel, that is, the lever which one uses to set the wheel spinning. Our mental roulette wheel is mounted at right angles to the ground, so put your fingers under the edge of your chair, and your thumb above and to the left, just as you would take hold of the right and left sides of the spar.

"Now give it a good flick as you pull your hand away, no wrist twisting, just the fingers giving the wheel a snappy twirl. Notice how the thumb crosses to the side of the index finger—naturally. The whole experience is similar to the feeling of the strings escaping the fingers when the stroke is done properly, that is, they escape quickly, smoothly, and simultaneously."

"Any reason you chóse a roulette wheel, don Diego?"

"Yes, it reminds me of guitar playing, Alfonso."

"In what sense?"

"You can't quit once you get the bug, and you're damned lucky if you make a *dime* at it. More likely, you'll go flat broke playing the damned thing!"

I laughed and he continued.

"Now we can try it out on the strings. I'll write out some examples, and I should like to comment on how they're written. You'll notice there is a complete separation between the rhythms done by the fingers (stems up) and the thumb (stems down). This two-part writing of the rhythm is a true reflection of the physical independence of thumb and fingers, which are now working much like the piano player's left and right hands.

"This may make the exercises look difficult to perform at first glance. But the matter is truly uncomplicated; there is only *one* question. The question is whether to pinch or not to pinch as your thumb ticks off the quarter note beats. The thumb keeps ticking, like a metronome, regardless of the action of the fingers. You see, the fingers are an option, the thumb is a necessity!

"Together now, Alfonso, let us count aloud. Keep the motion of the fingers neat and concise. One, two, three, four . . . ●

m = middle finger.
(from *medio* in Spanish)
a = ring finger.
(from *anular* in Spanish)

"This brings us to the point where I can sum up the essence of the Second Realm for you, Alfonso; pay attention. The thumb is the keeper of the beat, just as it was in the First Realm. The cornerstone of the Second Realm is the ability to keep the beat alive with a strong thumbstroke, directing it at individual strings, rather than all six. The fingers may then play notes on or off the beat, or not at all, but the thumbstroke must be as regular and forceful and automatic as foot-tapping. If it is, then the thumb and the fingers can work independently and you are a master of the technique of the Second Realm."

Don Diego paused to let this sink in.

"That's all there is to it, then?" I said appreciatively.

Don Diego laughed out loud. "That's all there is to it, Alfonso!"

We both laughed.

"But *can* you do it?" don Diego cut in to say. "Furthermore, can you do it while you make chord changes with your left hand? That is the question."

"Well, I don't know."

"Then let's find out," he said.

v. *The Music of the Second Realm*

"The chord change from C to G is about as easy as they come, wouldn't you agree, Alfonso?"

"Oh, very easy, all right."

"Then let's take the easiest right-hand pattern we can think of and put the two together. That way we can get a toehold in the music of the Second Realm.

"When I write this exercise I will use chord charts to show the left hand. The pointers under the chord charts show just where the chord begins.

"For the right hand I will use the staff to show the strings and the rhythm of their playing. *But* I am changing the heads of the notes to a diamond shape. This is because the notes are only being used to identify the strings, not the actual pitches. With chords in the left hand, the notes you hear will be different from those written, and I am rather strongly opposed to abusing this carefully wrought system of symbols, you see?"

"I see—but I have an alternative. Why not draw six lines for the six strings and put the notes on those? Then you won't compromise the system at all."

"Yes, yes, yes—what you describe is called *tablature.* However, our use of the staff is *transitional,* a jumping-off place for learning to read all the notes. The tablature system is a crutch; it is not good for learning to read music.

"Let's look at the exercise—can you play it?

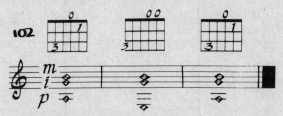

"I knew you wouldn't find that hard. It's quite all right to brace your ring finger against string one to make your hand more comfortable, as I see you are. ●

"Now have a look at this one, Alfonso."

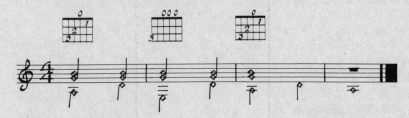

"Ah, not hard at all."

"Yes, but hold on a moment. Before you play, do the right hand by itself, playing just the open strings. Make sure you understand the rhythm, right? Two counts to the half note. ●

"Next, I suggest you play the thumb part by itself while changing chords. This emphasizes the cornerstone concept of the independent thumb. Then, finally, go ahead with the whole thing. ●

"I think you grasp the method now, Alfonso. I wrote these patterns in anticipation of today's lesson. We know the chords so well I just used C and G to indicate them. Practice the learning method as much as the music. First play the strings alone in rhythm, counting aloud. Second, play the thumb line by itself with the chords. Third, play it as written." ●

"What about this one, with the . . . triplets, right?"

"Yes, it is in 2/4 time, but each quarter note is subdivided into three pulses. You can do it easily—just say 'Me-xi-co, Me-xi-co; Me-xi-co, Me-xi-co' while you play, one Mexico to a foot tap. ●

"The next one requires a different approach. First I want you to tap your fingers in this pattern. ●

"Good, now play these notes with the thumb. ●

"I think you can guess the rest . . ." ●

vi. A Piece of the Second Realm

When I finished the last exercise I probably looked rather pleased with myself.

"Alfonso, think of the strides you have made in the last two weeks to be able to play like that—fine job, fine job. It's baffling to me that you would consider quitting now, just when you are beginning to pick up steam."

I was not particularly responsive. Don Diego took up another subject.

"Well, we're past the basics now, let's look at some real music."

I felt I should be firm. I put my guitar down inside the case.

"Don Diego, it's not fair of me to take up your time. You've explained the Second Realm to me, and you really have made it look simple. But . . ."

Don Diego was stirring up something very interesting on the

strings of his guitar. The music was not like anything we had played before, and yet it was—just far more melodious.

"What's that?"

"Eh? Oh, that's called a . . . a Venezuelan rag. It's the first piece I intended to show you."

"The first?"

"It's not hard, not at all—one picking pattern all the way, and all the chords are on the same four strings. The chords are exceedingly smooth in their connections, too. Here, I'll show you."

I reached down and picked up my guitar again.

"The first four chords have a clear pattern to them. While keeping the little finger pinned to the same spot on the first string, you march up the frets of the fourth, 1, 2, 3, with the index, middle, and ring finger.

"Then, while you're on the fourth chord you prepare the fifth by holding the index and middle finger over their targets. At the change you lower them quickly as you raise the ring finger.

"Anticipating our lesson today, I wrote them out with a much simpler picking pattern, just so you could get the rhythm of the changes. Try playing it . . . here, like so. ●

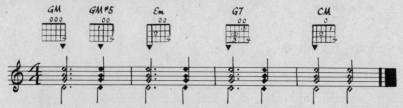

"For the first four bars then, the melody is in the bass. You will use your strong thumbstroke to make the bass line stand out. In bars five through eight, the melody is transferred up to the first string. You use a strong *finger*stroke to make *it* stand out.

"There is an interesting chord change at bar six. This unusual chord will be called 'high G major' for want of a better name—you see, as the chord chart shows, it consists of three open strings and the little finger planted on the seventh (VII) fret of string 1.

"To get to the high G chord from C-sharp diminished seven . . ."

"You come up with stranger names for chords all the time."

"Diminished is just another chord quality, like major, minor— that's all. A 'tangy' chord, eh? When you quit it, you release all the fingers except the little finger, which you use as a guide along string one to the seventh fret.

"The next chord, E minor 7, also in bar six, is all open strings."

"There's a tough one."

"I put it in so you'd have time to get your hand back to the first position again."

"Too bad you couldn't do that on the way up to high G. You can't make that slide without breaking rhythm, can you?"

"Perhaps not, but sometimes, if we're lucky, a tricky chord change will come at a place where we can slow the beat for dramatic effect."

"And we're lucky this time?"

"Right, this is the climax of the piece, so we can slow up a little on the last two eighth notes of C $\sharp$ diminished 7 and make the glide almost casually, robbing time as we please."

"Is that ethical—robbing time?"

"Oh, highly so. *Rubato* (roo-BAH-to), the Italian term for this liberal treatment of tempo, literally means 'robbed.' "

"How do you know all these terms, don Diego? I've been curious since the first lesson."

"Why did you hesitate to ask?"

"I don't know . . . just . . ."

"Anybody else might know them, but not an old fool gardener like me, eh?"

"No, I didn't think that, I . . ."

"How do you know the old man who owns the estate didn't hire a music teacher whom he put to work gardening in his spare time, eh?"

"Is that true, are you music teacher to the owner?"

Don Diego burst out laughing and slapped his knee.

"That old coot? Ha! You . . . you . . . I'm sorry Alfonso, you can't know what a joke that is. Let me tell you, the owner of this estate didn't get rich worrying about things like music. That guy cares about nothing except *money—money*, Alfonso—it's his lifeblood. And do you know how a man gets money like that old bastard's got in this country? Do you?"

"No," I said, awed by this tirade.

"Theft! Theft! That's how he gets it. Forget what you know about common decency; it's the rule of fang and claw. You don't make millions by being polite, Alfonso. You need a calculating mentality, able to dispense with emotional considerations completely. *Expediency* is the only moral code you can possibly maintain! What kind of guitar apprentice would such a person make, I ask you?! Music is the language of the emotions, Alfonso! That's what it is for me—for the likes of that old badger it's a decoration, a soothing sound. It's like the carpet you walk on!"

"Why do you work for him, if that's the way you feel?"

"Gotta eat, Alfonso, gotta eat." He suddenly seemed deflated.

"Besides," he added, "I go my way, and he goes his. But to answer your original question—music was in the family. My father was a church organist and choir instructor."

"Oh."

"In Barquisimeto. I'd rather not go into that now, though—we're almost done. Reach for that high note in G major 9 while you're still playing D7, and, huh . . . I think that's all for the left hand.

"So, please play these bars, picking the four strings at once in the rhythm I've indicated. Let's do it a few times. ●

"Having finished with the left hand, let's take care of the right. First, just the fingers, learn to tap the pattern on the table. Count aloud, Alfonso, and let your fingers exaggerate the accents on one and, to a lesser extent, on three." ●

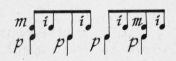

He placed a new piece of paper in front of the old.

A VENEZUELAN RAG

"Here is the whole thing. As you read the picking pattern of the strings you will find the thumb playing 3, 4, 3, 4 in the first bar, then 4, 3, 4, 3 becomes the rule.

"In the seventh bar you begin to slow down gradually. The 'rit.' sign shows you where to begin. It stands for *ritardando*, (ree-tar-DAHN-do), another Italian term. The slowing down is very pronounced by the end. The last note should be given out like the last drop of wine—you don't want to admit the bottle is empty, but you don't want to wait too long for it to arrive either."

He took the music paper off the stand and handed it to me. I took it and looked at it briefly, then dropped it in my guitar case.

"Once you've memorized the chords, you'll have no trouble playing it professionally," said don Diego, watching me put the guitar in over the paper. "There is much more, of course, much more to the Second Realm."

"Thanks, don Diego," I answered, sitting upright. "Thanks very much for this lesson. It's been very enlightening, and I'd gladly take more lessons, er, that is, stay with the apprenticeship, but there's always that drive to and from Caracas hanging over my head, and the things waiting there for me to do. The fact is that I can't do justice to your teaching—I just can't."

Surprisingly, don Diego smiled. "Well, if you can't, amigo, then you can't, right? Ha!" he exclaimed, clapping both hands against his thighs. He got up from his chair smiling, and with hands clasped behind his back he went to the window and looked out. I latched up the guitar case.

When I looked up don Diego's expression had changed. He seemed very serious and contemplative. The afternoon light shone into his face and he squinted.

"There's one more thing you should hear before you take the walk back."

"Does it have to do with guitar?"

"Oh no, no—not guitar."

"What then?"

"Perhaps it's nothing, but all the same, it's possible . . ." Diego paused for several moments.

"What's possible?" I asked.

"It's possible—that your life is in danger!"

vii. *A Letter—A Week and a Half Later*

Dear Melinda:

It was a pleasure to hear from you so soon after sending the tapes. Sorry my research turned up only "stock Latin American jug band," music, though. I couldn't tell the difference.

On the other hand, it was great to know I made at least "one discovery really worth pursuing." That was a surprise since Diego de Luna was the one discovery from whom you never heard a single note.

However, I see why you're interested, since it gave you the idea for your thesis—"Ethnic Approaches to Musical Pedagogy—A Cross-cultural Survey." Sounds very interesting, and I'd love to help you out.

I'm afraid, though, I have some bad news to break to you. I quit taking lessons from de Luna almost two weeks ago. Another thing is, one has suspicions as to how 'ethnic' he really is—he has a vocabulary like a music professor, and he is a sophisticated actor. His ethnicity could be a put-on.

For example, at the end of our last lesson, right after I quit, he informs me suddenly that a jaguar has moved into the territory, and to protect my life, he will escort me down the mountain. This turned out to be a pretext for a lecture designed to get me back into the apprenticeship. The lecture started when he remarked on the beauty, noble spirit, and wisdom of the jaguar. I told him I agreed on the first count, but given the jaguar's tendency to eat people, I didn't know about the latter two. He asked me if I had ever heard of a deceitful jaguar, or one who was not at home with nature and himself.

Well, the conversation was a long one, but the upshot of it was that the virtuosity of a player was secondary to the quality of his spirit. So cultivating the spirit is the proper role of a teacher—the rest will follow in due course.

I don't know if there ever really was a jaguar, or if he just wanted to keep me off balance. It's a Madison Avenue technique, you know—using fear to accompany the sales pitch. That's a pretty sophisticated subterfuge, isn't it?

As I write I'm recalling your words and I know you must be sorry you can't follow through on it yourself just yet. And to tell the truth, I wanted to know more about the old character, too. I'll tell you what —I'll see what can be done. It depends on whether I can harmonize it with school. I'm not doing well this quarter for some reason.

I'll keep you posted. And this time, I'll get a tape—for sure.

Love,
Al

LESSON IV:

Return to the Second Realm

i. A Confrontation

From within the cabin came the sound of feet padding across a wooden floor. The tarnished metal knob rotated and the door opened a crack.

Diego de Luna squinted out from the cave-like interior into the glaring light of day. He raised a pair of sunglasses to eye level, holding them about a foot before his face.

"Well, well—if it isn't Alfonso. That explains everything."

"What do you mean?"

"The tea . . . would you like some tea?"

"Why yes, I would."

"That verifies it, then. I haven't brewed any tea this time of day for weeks, what with the heat and all."

Don Diego was up and moving as he spoke. In the closet-sized kitchen a tea kettle was just beginning to whistle.

". . . so when a voice said 'make tea' to me, I knew something was afoot."

"What voice is that?" I asked.

"Same one that warns you not to run through a stop sign on a deserted road when there's a cop hiding around the corner, Alfonso."

Don Diego came striding back with two cups and a steaming pot. Like everything else he owned except his guitar, they were well worn, if not antiquated. The metal teapot was dented and its handle was wrapped, half in bamboo and half by a brown shoelace cleverly braided and knotted through the hinge.

"Now, my friend," said de Luna, pouring, "to what do I owe the honor of your presence?"

"Well, don Diego, let me toss a question back at you in reply— have you opened that bottle of wine I brought you two weeks ago? The one you said you were going to save until I'd finished the Three Realms?"

"Not yet."

"Good, because I've decided I want to continue on the path that leads up to that bottle of wine. That's why I'm back."

"Then you want to resume your study of the Three Realms?"

"I want to make it to the very top of the third peak."

"Well, this is quite a turnabout. Something must have happened —did they smarten up, perhaps, and boot you out of school?"

"No, no."

"A-ha, *you* wised up and quit—now you want to study something worthwhile!"

"You mean, study the art of guitar playing?"

"Right," said he.

"Well, yes and no, actually. I certainly want to study the art of guitar, but nothing's changed at school, not really."

"Nothing changed? Nothing? Pardon me for questioning your judgment, but if you are as burdened as ever with schoolwork, how can you possibly undertake the discipline of a guitar apprenticeship? You said it was too much for you before."

"I know, I know. But there are reasons."

I sipped at the tea for a moment's space. "There are two reasons, one of which could involve considerable benefits for you, don Diego."

"Oh?"

"Yes. Well, first and foremost, don Diego, I'm the kind of person who likes to see a job through to the end. Here I'd come as far as the Second Realm of Guitar Knowledge, only to quit—it grated on my conscience."

Don Diego frowned.

"And the other reason, one I think you'll find intriguing, is that, well, this takes some explaining."

"I'm listening."

"My musicologist friend—you know, the one in the U.S. who wanted me to record the folk musicians for her when I got down here?"

"Yes?"

"She's heard about you through me . . ."

"Yes?" Don Diego's left brow shot up.

"And . . . and she'd like to make a special study of you."

Don Diego got up and began walking back and forth with his hands clasped behind his back.

"I see. And how is this going to be beneficial to me?"

"You see, Melinda . . ."

"Your girlfriend?"

"Uh no, not really—wouldn't mind it though."

"I see, go on."

"It seems Melinda is in a position to carry your music to some very influential people. She could generate a lot of interest in you. Who knows, it could put you on the road to fame and fortune!"

"What makes her think I'm so interesting?"

"I told her about our first lesson. She only knows about your music by my description, but she's already suggested that she would make the trip down here to interview you personally!"

"Hmm."

Don Diego's lack of response was perturbing.

"Do you realize what this could mean to you, don Diego? No more working for a boss you don't like, travel—some big changes!"

"Yes, I realize very well. One question: Does Melinda know the name of my town yet?"

"No."

"Good."

"Good?"

"That's what I said—good!" don Diego growled. Then, resuming his pacing, he said in a tone that reminded me of my first encounter with him, "I don't want her to know any more about me—nothing—not the name of my town, not a note of my music!"

"Not your music? It could be your big break, though, the beginning of a better life for you."

"Don't be patronizing! I said no—not one inch of tape. . . ." He patted the breast pockets of his coat. ". . . Not even my brand of cigar."

Don Diego pulled out a muddy green cigar and bit off the end. He spat it out.

"I don't understand," I said as he lit up.

"You don't have to understand. It's what I request, that's enough."

"Well, I hope you're not mad."

"Mad, no; I am disappointed."

"But you never required that I keep the lessons or your identity a secret!"

"I never thought you, a chemist, could tell anyone who would be in a position to stir up trouble. It never occurred to me to mention secrecy to you. I thought you would understand. And I am disappointed—disappointed in the reasons you have for coming back. You say you want to finish something you started? Why?! You are not *obligated* to finish the Three Realms! It is an adventure, but you sound like you are being a good clerk keeping up his tidy habits. And, you put the most important reason last—the girl, you want to *use* me to please a girl you like!"

"No."

"You could be very attractive to women, young man, without running around doing favors for them at their beck and call."

"I don't—I wasn't!"

"Then maybe you thought you could profit some other way—promoting my career as a performer?"

At this my hackles rose.

"That accusation is absurd! Look, I'll admit liking Melinda and that wanting to do something helpful for her influenced my decision, but I see no reason to apologize for that! It was *also* her opinion of you. She said your teaching approach was novel, charming, and profoundly interesting. In fact, she said you were a 'priceless discovery.' She did all she could to persuade me to continue, for my own sake as much as for hers!"

"Hmmpf." Don Diego emitted a puff of smoke.

"As for hoping to profit from selling your music to some recording company—the thought just plain never entered my head! Even what Melinda said wasn't enough."

"What was it, then?"

"A . . . a *realization.* It took me two weeks, but when I woke up in my rabbit warren of an apartment this morning and looked out at the smog, the balance tipped. I realized I could not do without having this sanctuary to get away to. There's a sense of mystery and wonder I have about the Three Realms that I wish I had about everything."

"*Sí,*" assented don Diego, staring out the window and puffing.

"That's the reason I've come up here—there's got to be a place where I can breathe freely for a while and rejuvenate my spirit. I realized that learning the Three Realms is a spiritual *necessity*—that's why I'm back, that's why I want to finish, and not some 'clerical habit!' "

Don Diego turned his head toward me and cocked an eyebrow. He looked rather like a wise old crow.

"These words are . . . unexpected coming from you, Alfonso. But, because there is real emotion in them, you cause me to reconsider. I am glad you came after all—and glad to accept you back as a guitar apprentice."

"Thank you, don Diego."

"Have you practiced at all in the last two weeks?"

"I learned the Venezuelan rag."

"Play it for me, then."

ii. *Second Half of the Second Realm*

By the time we embarked on new material don Diego was in fine fettle, and we were conversing as amiably as we ever had before.

"By your execution of the Venezuelan rag I see you have an excellent grasp of the technique of the Second Realm, and your spirit is taking charge of the expressive elements, too. It remains, then, to amplify your *mental* powers. When you have filled the Five Gaps you will be ready to enter the Third Realm of Guitar Knowledge."

"What are the Five Gaps?"

"Ask *where*, not what, Alfonso! They are here, between the strings!"

So saying, don Diego dropped his thumb across string 6 and then 5. "You know these notes, E and A, but not the notes in between."

"F and G!"

"Filled, the First Gap reads: E–F–G–A. To fill the Second Gap, A to D, you need B and C—A–B–C–D. What is the Third?"

"D to G; you need E and F."

"Right."

"Well, it shouldn't take too long to handle those, don Diego—show me the first one."

"I wish it were that easy. If we take them on in order, I, II, III, this results in an empty intellectual exercise. Look, here they are, all five filled brim full . . .

"But does it have any meaning to you? There is no myth behind this constellation—a bunch of stars with no story to show the links! We must enter the Five Gaps in a way that stimulates all the faculties —the senses, imagination, mind, soul!

○ explored
● unexplored

iii. *The Story of the Five Gaps*

"OK, what can you feel for a bunch of notes?"

"Good question. Let's start by giving them an identity. Alfonso, shake hands with the *natural notes*."

"Natural, as opposed to *un*natural?"

"Uh, no—natural, as in pristine, unaltered—as in the white keys of the piano, too, by the way. The white keys are naturals."

"White—pure, natural."

"Remember that, amigo, use your imagination to give the natural notes a *white* feeling. As you memorize the locations tag them white in your mind's eye. This will benefit you later, in the Third Realm.

"Now, just as people have a name and a job, so the notes named natural have a job too—they make up the C major scale."

"Do they ever change jobs?"

"Yes, but one job at a time, eh? We shall focus on learning the C major scale. Now, from the scale we can make many chords. But the C major chord is primary. Why? Because it captures the fundamental harmony which is the mother of all the scale tones. It is home base in the key of C, do you follow?"

"Go on."

"All our lines of thought seem to converge on the C chord, so let us begin to fill the Five Gaps there. It makes an extremely simple starting point—only four notes on four strings:

"Though simple, it is very rich, Alfonso, because between the top and bottom C notes of the chord, we can find a complete scale, Do, Re, Mi, Fa, Sol . . ."

"La, Ti, Do."

"Very good."

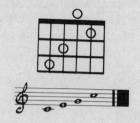

iv. Filling the Five Gaps

Don Diego was writing out notes with lightning rapidity as he spoke.

"We'll put all that Second Realm technique you've acquired to use now, Alfonso. This is a drill for identifying the notes of the C chord. There is no rhythm and no tempo; it is all a matter of recognizing the notes. But it is also a matter of communication between your brain and your fingers. The dotted bar line helps you keep track of where you are. ●

"Now we shall add the element of rhythm." ●

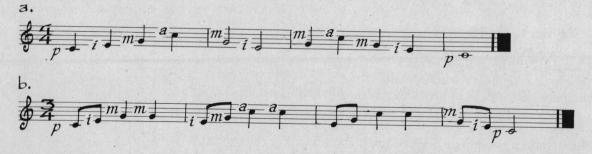

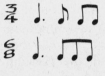

When we came to the fifth exercise, don Diego had some special instruction.

"If I recollect properly, this marks your first experience with 6/8 time, Alfonso."

"I think you're right."

"The unit of the beat in 6/8 time is the dotted quarter note. That is, 6/8 does *not* usually mean six beats of eighth notes, it means two beats of three eighth notes each."

"I wonder if you could make that more graphic for me."

"Take this for example . . . (*See drawing at right.*)"

"Are the note values the same?"

"A dotted quarter, three eighth notes—yeah, they're the same."

"Right, however, in the 3/4 version, the dot represents the first half of the second beat, see?"

"Check."

"Whereas in the 6/8 version—since there are three eighth notes to each beat—the dot is part of the first beat. The count on the 3/4 version is 'one–(two)–and-three-and.' For the 6/8 it is, 'one-nn-nn, two-oo-oo.'"

"With all this detail, don Diego, I wonder if I can *play* the darn thing."

"That will be no problem, the feeling of exercise 5 is already familiar to you—it is like triplets in 2/4 time."

"Me-xi-co, Me-xi-co?"

"Sí. ●

"Alfonso, I appreciate your forbearance."

"How so?"

"Don't tell me you wouldn't like a change of chords by now?"

"Well yes, it would be nice to hear a G chord too, now and then."

"Good instincts, my friend! Then add this note, G, third fret, string 6, and we'll have a G chord to play with.

"Play C, then, G, then C, please, Alfonso. ●

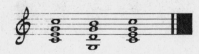

"What do you hear?"

"Hmm . . . relaxation, tension, relaxation, maybe?"

"Good observation. There is a polarity in the harmony, as there was in the beat. In C there is a sense of repose, in G a sense of activity or motion.

"Play G, then C, then G—listen . . ." ●

"It sounds unfinished, incomplete."

"Yes, until the C chord is played we are in suspense. The G chord pulls strongly toward the C."

"Like gravity."

"In music this gravity is called *tonality!*"

"Gravity theories interest me don Diego, but if I succeed in filling the Five Gaps today, won't that be enough?"

"Quite right, Alfonso. You can think of tonality as synonymous with key, if you like, and we'll go on studying the C scale through the Five Gaps."

"Wait a minute now—I'd like to know the difference between key and scale, if any—that's what I'd like."

"Oh, there is a difference. In the C scale there are just seven notes. In the key of C, however, we find the scale notes, the chords made from the notes, and even some notes and chords not in the scale. In a key there is a central tone, a home base, and it can be glorified with all kinds of procedures. But a scale remains a fixed formula, certain notes allowed, and that's all."

"Interesting."

"Some scenery along the way, Alfonso."

Then don Diego began writing out exercises, and I started playing them as he wrote.

"Hey, these are the same as the ones you taught me two weeks ago."

"Shows what a rut my mind is in—I'll add a couple of new ones."

a.

b.

c.

MASTERING GUITAR

d.

e.

v. A Slur upon the Guitar

"These notes, F and A, finish filling out the scale."

"Then are we ready to play some tunes?"

"Almost. As soon as we start to play melodies we're going to run into the slur mark and I think we'd better take care of that first."

"Is the slur a technique?"

"Yes, it imitates a singer changing notes on one syllable—La-aa-aa, instead of La-La-La. It involves dropping a left hand finger on a vibrating string like a velvet hammer, or pulling the finger forcefully away from a fretted string like a bull pawing the earth. In either case the aim is to pass the vibration along the string as you change frets with the left hand, with no help from the right hand after the first note."

"Oh yes, I've used those for a long time—called them hammer-on and pull-off."

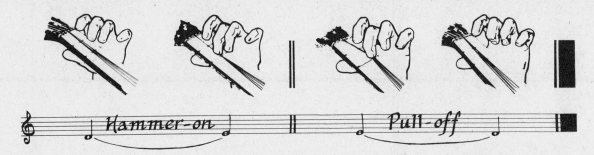

"If you know them, then play this for me, Alfonso."

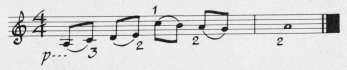

A *slur* looks like a tie, but the tie connects *identical* notes, while the slur connects *different* notes.

"Very good. Once more, this time slower and tapping your foot. We want to make our timing impeccable."

vi. Scale Play

"Do you think you can play the scale now, Alfonso—C to C?"

"*Sí, sí,* of course." ●

"How about a descending scale with slurs? Careful to prepare the E in bar 3.

"Not bad. But I notice a tendency to make the beat coincide with the slurring finger, instead of the other way around! Try again—attune your ears to the beat, and let the *beat* hold your fingers and move them. ●

"Well done, Alfonso. However, once you start skipping around from note to note as one must in melodies, it gets a little trickier. Try playing this row of notes—I think you'll see what I mean. No tempo and no rhythm here, just find each note and play it." ●

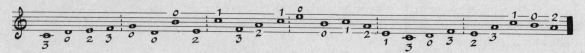

Though he had an ear on my playing, don Diego was scribbling something new at the same time.

"What do you have there?" I asked.

"Another sort of reading problem—two notes at once. Try to take in both notes at the blink of an eye, if you can."

"That's hard."

"Now—but soon you'll digest a stack of four at once, like pancakes."

"How can you do that?!"

"You run across the same combinations so often, they begin to look like chord charts. ●

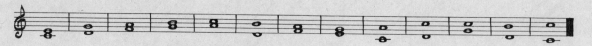

"What does your eye see here, Alfonso?"

a.

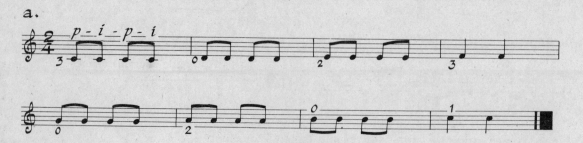

b.

"A lot of notes."

"Come on, think."

"Sure, it's just the scale again, but notes are being repeated."

"Right. Always look for patterns in the music. Patterns are the glue one uses to stick together hundreds of notes in one's memory. ●

"In order to play melodies it is necessary to be able to play scale skips such as these quite smoothly and unhesitatingly."

a.

b.

c.

d.

vii. *Hearing the Song in the Guitar*

"This is your first tune. Give it a try."

"How's that, don Diego?"

"You got all the notes, Alfonso, but not the proper feeling. A song is not done like an exercise! Don't play the notes one by one—play the bars, in fact, play every four bars as if they were of a piece."

"What do you mean by that?"

"This tune, like many others, is made of four-bar phrases. That is, there is a single idea unifying each group of four bars, and a slackening of drive where the ideas end."

"Well, what does that mean in terms of performance?"

"A singer interprets with *emotion*. This is a combination of rhythmic feeling, dynamics, and tone color. You can do the same on your guitar."

"Sounds complicated."

"It is—when you start talking about it. I don't want to explain it to you, though. I want you to discover how it works through struggling to make your guitar sing."

"To make my guitar sing . . . hmm."

"By singing as you play."

"But my singing is terrible."

"Doesn't matter—you teach your guitar to sing as you would *want* to sing yourself."

"Do I have to?"

"Listen, to sing with your guitar and lead it with your voice is the beginning of thoughtful playing. If you learn to hear and create a singing voice in your guitar, you have made it an extension of your own soul, rather than a machine for making notes. Don't you think that is desirable?"

"Yes."

"Good. Now please, sing each phrase on one breath, and try to imagine an identical flow of breath in your guitar."

"Wait! Uh, I don't know the right way to do the dynamics, and stuff like that."

"Alfonso, persnickety artist though I am, you have my full permission to do what you will with my tune. You can sing it like a Caruso or like a drunkard leaning on a lamppost—you may even add notes of your own—as long as you try to make your guitar sing with the same spirit!" ●

"This is the second tune I have written for today."

"Hmm, all chords . . . and what are these (⌢) marks?"

"A *fermata* (fayr-MAH-ta) means a pause—in effect, to hold the notes one and a half times their written value."

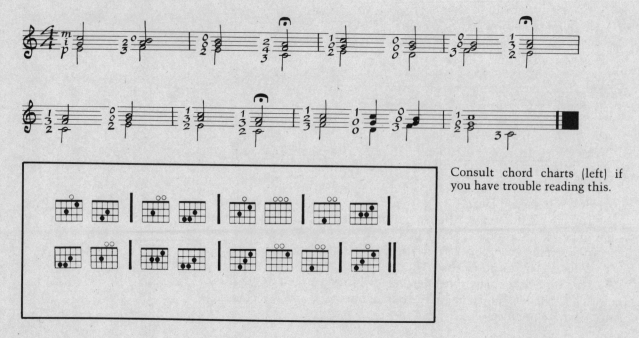

Consult chord charts (left) if you have trouble reading this.

viii. A Lesson In Fortune-Telling

Don Diego stood up and stretched.

"How about some more tea, my friend?"

"Sounds good—I could use a break."

While don Diego pumped up his gas stove and put the water on, I wandered outside. A breeze was up and the mountain air had turned cool. Though we were only a mile or so from town and ostensibly on the grounds of a baronial estate, there was a wild and primitive atmosphere to don Diego's habitat. There was nothing in view except primeval forest, nothing audible but the birds and the wind-rustled foliage.

At this point I began to wonder if scanning the scenery behind don Diego's might not disclose some sign of the estate house—an exposed roof, a chimney, a puff of smoke among the trees.

I walked around the cabin and took in the panorama with a searching eye. The land played tricks on your perceptions, as it often will, not letting you see just how minute you are and how enormous it is, until you venture to go up near it. Directly beyond the level clearing, the slope began to rise and ripple dramatically. To the left and right above the treetops was a sweeping view of many miles of mountain ridge. The hills became increasingly steeper and more convoluted toward the crest of the ridge, with some vertical outcroppings of bare rock amid the hardy vegetation.

But there was no clear-cut boundary to the skyline. Instead, herds of fluffy white clouds had settled down over the peaks, obscuring the higher regions in a chilly gray mistiness. Shards of vapor poured through the hollows, dissipating like steam when they hit some invisible boundary line in the air.

The tufted carpet of broadleaved trees tilted skyward with the mountainside, faithfully clinging to every contour. My eyes wandered high and low over this spectacularly beautiful landscape but nowhere was there evidence of any human habitation.

I decided to walk farther out and explore the clearing, perhaps to find the path that don Diego used to come and go from work. I had taken a few steps when suddenly the forest went dead silent except for the lonely sounds of the wind stirring branches and whispering through the leaves. Don Diego's warning about the jaguar flooded my brain and the hair stood up on the back of my neck. I turned around and hurried back to the cabin, keeping an eye out over my shoulder.

When I came inside he was standing by the table, pouring hot water into the teapot.

"Ah, Alfonso, I wondered where you had gone."

"Just looking around outside."

"Find anything interesting?"

"The birds stopped singing all of a sudden just now."

Don Diego nodded his head.

"Well, might mean something. We may have a guest on the way."

"The jaguar, do you think?"

"The jaguar? Might be. But it may mean nothing at all."

"You're not concerned?"

"No."

"Why not?"

"I think the jaguar has a distinct preference for guitar students over stringy old gardeners. Here, let's sit down outside, maybe he'll show up."

"You want me to be the bait?! I'll pass on that."

"Don't let it bother you. I'll get my rifle, and you can have the pistol."

"No, no . . . It's just too sunny out there."

"Perhaps you're right," said don Diego, glancing out the window and squinting. "Clouds are staying on the mountain. Well, I don't know about you, but I'm going to sit on the floor; I need a change of backrests."

Don Diego put the pillow from his bed against the wall, sat down and drew his knees up to his chest. I brought my teacup over and sat near the other wall, under the window. The Venezuelan sunlight streamed through the glass and fell warm and soothing across my back.

"That last piece we played, don Diego . . ."

"Yes?"

"It sounded like church music."

"So it did. It was in the style of a hymn."

"Did you learn to write like that in some school, or was it from your father?"

"My father."

"Did he teach you the guitar, too?"

"No, no—what a bizarre notion!" He paused. "My father thought the guitar was for the peasantry. Though they mainly played a four-string guitar, called the *quatro*."

"Then where did you learn to play?"

"You want to know the whole story, eh?" he said, looking over at me.

"I sure would, I mean, if you don't mind."

"No, but you realize how tiresome old men can be when they start talking about their past, don't you?"

"I don't expect your past to be tiresome."

"Very well, then, to begin at the beginning, my father was a methodical, religious sort of man, and he taught music in a large church in Barquisimeto. He was choir conductor and played the organ for the congregation on Sundays and holidays, at weddings, funerals, and so forth. He also tutored violin. There's a lot of dancing and festivities in Barquisimeto. Did you know that?"

"No."

"Traditional. But he never cared much for it. He had higher standards. We were poor, but he held his head above the rest because he had 'culture.' He was a very serious, disciplined man, and stuck in his ways. Stuck in his position, too, and he knew it. He was not a young father. And he already had a career picked out for me before I came along, Alfonso."

"What was that, don Diego?"

"Musical prodigy."

"So he was going to live out his own frustrated dream of success through you?"

"Ahhh . . . I would not oversimplify. But that is partly right. When I came along, I was pushed hard. And I was not without qualifications for the position. I had an unerring ear, a good memory, agile hands for a youngster. I was a fast learner. When I showed an interest in composing, he taught me harmony and counterpoint. But I didn't dare imitate the music I heard out in the streets. This is not to say I disliked the classics—but try as he could, Alfonso, the old man could not make a little Mozart of me. I wasn't good enough—not with just one teacher, one I resented.

"The big change came when my mother died. In spite of his professed beliefs, the old man took to drink."

Don Diego stopped short. I had been settling into a more relaxed position, and my foot had accidentally toppled my teacup. The puddle began to spread. Several liquid branches were growing ominously.

"Uh, I'm sorry, don Diego, tell me where a rag is and I'll take care of this mess."

I was getting nervous because he was looking sideways at the puddle with a jeweler's eye.

"Don't bother," said don Diego, and he went to the cabinet, returning with a small paint brush.

"Here, while I talk, you paint."

"Paint? Paint what?"

"See what you can find in that puddle, some sort of image."

"I'd rather not."

"It's the price I ask for my story."

"Well, OK . . . I guess."

"What will you find in there, Alfonso? Eh? Tea monsters? Don't laugh. There's something for you in there, I believe. Don't disregard this opportunity."

"Opportunity? What do you mean?" (It looked like an entirely standard wet puddle to me.)

"A tea puddle, especially an uncontrived tea puddle, is a very good place to find a reflection of fate. Since it was your fortune to make that pool of tea, that pool of tea is saturated with your fortune!"

"Or maybe it's that old gypsy's idea of a Rorschach test," I thought as he went for his guitar. He sat down and resumed his story, accompanying his words with improvised music.

"I was about fourteen when I first heard the radio broadcast from Caracas."

"Which broadcast was that?"

"The first, man! I was born about the time the last dinosaur died, Alfonso."

"A-ha, I see."

"Well, they were playing big-city music, Alfonso. I heard it and I was infected. I decided to run away, and for once I knew better than to ask for permission! The old man woke up one morning and I was gone. So were the contents of the cookie jar."

"So you're a thief in addition to other accomplishments."

"I left an I.O.U. I'm no thief."

I swirled the brush idly, encouraging the currents to dance to the music and cursed the luck that prevented me from getting the tape recorder out of my pack immediately and saving the whole performance for Melinda. Then I leaned on my side and propped my head on my elbow. I didn't see don Diego, I only heard his voice and his guitar as I became absorbed in painting the puddle.

"So I arrived in Caracas. And there was little pity in that town, Alfonso. I was robbed the same day I arrived. There would have been something fitting about that, if I hadn't left the I.O.U! I was in despair, but I would sooner have died than go back home, sniveling and pleading for forgiveness to the triumph of my father.

"So I went to a restaurant and offered to play piano. The owner said no, but he gave me a loaf of bread. I went to several others—nothing. Then, at another one, they sat me down for an audition. I began to play Beethoven. But they stopped me immediately. Didn't I know anything popular? I played from the folk music I knew, but even that, they said, was outdated and 'hick stuff.' So I got off the stool and began to walk out. I planned on going to the nearest bridge and jumping off. But then I heard some whispers, and one man said, 'Hey, can you play guitar?' And of course I lied and said I could.

"I guess they thought anyone who could play piano like I could could surely strum the guitar, and I was hired without an audition. The show was that night, some three hours away. I went to a music store a few blocks away and rented a guitar with the last of my money. I also managed to stash an instruction book in the case before I left—desperate circumstances require desperate remedies, Alfonso. I devoured as much of those pages as I could in the time remaining and, believe it or not, absorbed enough to fake it through that evening.

"Was I good? No! I was terrible, terrible, Alfonso. But I learned the first task of the apprentice guitarist that way—the hard way. The band leader, he took me aside afterward, and by all the signs I knew I was going to get the axe, so I cried and I spilled my whole, miserable story to him. He was sympathetic, and he even took some time right then and there to show me some things about playing the guitar. That was my first break, Alfonso. And that's when I took up with what my father called The Instrument of the Devil.

"I remember some of the songs from those days. Like this one . . ."

The song don Diego sang had a restless rhythm, but the melody was slow, minor, and forlorn, and don Diego's mind seemed to be a long ways away.

When the verses were done he began humming improvisations on the tune, and as his voice and his guitar interwove their lines, a fantasy of a man and a woman dancing entered my mind. They held each other and danced wherever the tip of my brush led them.

My head and shoulders blocked the sunlight coming from behind me and cast a crisp, dark shadow over my tea painting. As I maneuvered the brush my mind became increasingly engrossed in that patch of night. Then, as if it were a darkened theatre, a curtain drew back and I saw my fantasy projected on a stage within: a lamplit courtyard sometime 'after two,' the pair of lovers oblivious to all but each other, dancing to the music of a guitarist who sits in the shadows.

Around and around they waltzed and my eyelids grew heavier and heavier. The courtyard scene dwindled in size as the wind outside the cabin seemed to grow louder. Don Diego's guitar grew fainter, hushed.

I breathed deep, relaxed breaths and heard nothing but wind in trees, nor did I see anything but inky darkness. That was all—silence and darkness.

Silence! Had the jaguar come after all?! I sat up suddenly and blinked, but the darkness refused to be dispelled. I stared with my eyes wide open in confusion. Where the tea puddle had been now lay the smoldering coals of a campfire, and instead of a cabin, I was surrounded on all sides by forest. I looked over my shoulder. A crescent moon was high overhead, and the pale light of the stars fell across the tops of the trees, only to be choked off before reaching the ground.

Suddenly, I was aware of a presence. I was not alone. There was something nearby, something alien and powerful, and moving, moving quietly toward me.

There was a stick in my hand. Fire! I needed fire! I had to have light! I thrust the stick into the coals and stirred frantically. The flame kicked up, and in the shower of sparks I saw, not ten feet away, broadside and pacing, the golden coat and glowing eyes of the jaguar.

"No!" I screamed, "No! Get away!"

"No!" I heard myself yelling as I awakened, waving my arms and lurching out toward the dozing don Diego.

He jumped up like a startled jack rabbit, crying "Jesus!" as his guitar flew out of his lap. With a wild stab he snatched it out of midair. He fell back onto his pillow with a thud, and held his hand over his pounding heart.

"Bad . . . dream, eh . . . Alfonso?" he panted.

I was still rubbing my eyes. My leg felt clammy and cold. I looked down, and my pants were soaked with tea. I had lunged right into it.

"Yeah, bad dream, I guess."

"You guess?! My god, I hope that's not how you always wake up from your naps!"

"Sorry, sorry." I yawned and then said, "Try to look on the bright side of it, don Diego. The tea mess is more or less taken care of now."

"What was that dream about, Alfonso—if I may ask, seeing that it was my heart that almost burst as a result of it?"

"Let me think." (I didn't want to say.)

"Must have been gruesome."

"Gruesome? Hmm, yeah. A nightmare of the worst proportions. I dreamed Dr. Forzosa was playing guitar and singing. Horrible!"

"Dr. Forzosa? Should I know him?"

"He's a character in a horror film."

"Oh, I see why I haven't heard of him—I don't go to the movies."

"You're lucky you never saw that one, anyway."

Don Diego looked at the smear on the floor. I was trying to wring out my pants leg.

"I don't suppose you found an image in the tea, did you, Alfonso?"

"Well, yes, as a matter of fact I did."

"Excellent! Tell me, what was it?"

"Just before I fell asleep, I saw a couple, two lovers, dancing in a Spanish courtyard by lamplight. It was late, and they were the only ones there, except for a guitar player."

"How would you describe their dancing?"

"Effortless, weightless."

"That," said don Diego, "is a very good price for my story."

ix. Finishing the Five Gaps

Don Diego said we were done with the lion's share of the work and we could now finish filling the Five Gaps without any trouble.

"We have the trunk; now let's get the limbs—the bass side first. When we add F and B, our knowledge will be complete.

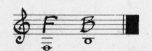

"Now see how you do identifying all the notes you know so far. Just point to them on your guitar and say their name. While you practice, I will write. ●

"This *arpeggio* study employs almost all the C notes we have learned so far."

"Excuse me; ar-PEJ-o?"

"Italian for harp-like. An arpeggio is a chord whose notes are played in succession rather than all at once. It is sometimes called a broken chord."

"Then the style of the Second Realm is an arpeggio style?"

"True enough."

"And the Third Realm, what is that?"

Don Diego looked at me poker-faced.

"Right. Let me see if I can play this." ●

"With these three notes,

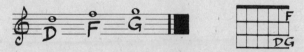

See below for chord chart assistance.

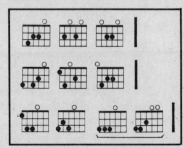

"... we complete the filling of the Five Gaps. String 1 has the same notes as string 6, you'll notice, since both strings are tuned to E.

"We'll take some time to become acquainted with these new notes before we play the three melodies which stress them. I will call out notes from these two strings, and you simply point to them, all right?

"C-B-D-G| E-F-D-C| D-B-G-D| E-C-B-F| G-D-F-C| E-G-C-F| E-C.

"And now a string of notes to be played, without rhythm. ●

"Here are two more melodies, my friend."

"The first one looks straightforward enough," I observed.

"Yes, and it should be played at a brisk tempo. Now let's look at the last tune. The first tune I gave you today (page 87) was in the key of C major. The one we just discussed was in A minor. Now this last one uses *both* keys. It works because A minor and C major are closely related keys, in fact we say they are relatives—C major is the *relative major* of A minor, and? Please?"

"A minor is the relative minor of C major?"

"Exactly so."

"Very interesting, but can it help me play guitar?"

"Not five minutes from now, certainly—but in the Second Domain of Guitar Knowledge, yes. Let us look now at the *form* of this piece. It is a very common form for songs and dances: A:A:B:A, eight bars in each section, 32 bars in all. This has been the prevailing form in popular music ever since I can remember, Alfonso."

"What does '*D.C. al fine*' mean?"

"Dah-KAH-po ahl FEE-nay means to repeat the composition from the beginning up to the word *fine,* which means 'end.' The repeat mark gives you A:A. Then you play the B section once and, da capo, go to the top again—A:A:B:A."

x. *The Five Gaps in Review*

"Well, Alfonso, the Five Gaps are filled, we've reached our goal."

"Have we ever. I had no idea there was so much to it."

"Let's not overdo the complexity of it, my friend. Allow me to review how we know the notes to give us a perspective.

"First of all, we know them in a physical sense, through our sense of touch and our ability to play them where and when and how fast we want.

"We know them in a mental sense on a string-by-string basis as names and locations . . .

names . . . and

"The whole pattern becomes more memorable, as I have shown you, by relating the notes to the shadow of the well-known C chord. Now, beyond touch and sight, there is yet a third way, in which we know the scale."

"What is this way?"

locations . . .

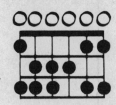

"Knowledge of the sounds of the notes in the shadow of the scale. This is most important—without this knowledge the rest is dry and lifeless."

"Well, how can I learn that?"

"If you want to develop this knowledge, you should begin by playing all the simplest songs you can think of, nursery rhymes or what have you, carefully avoiding stepping outside of the shadow of the scale."

"What if the tunes aren't in the key of C?"

"Doesn't matter—listen for the *sound* of the tune."

"Give me an example."

"Take . . . take 'Twinkle, Twinkle, Little Star.' "

"Oh come on."

"No! It's a good one to start with!"

"You see? Now, Alfonso, if it is so terribly easy for you, I challenge you to play 'Twinkle Twinkle Little Star' yourself, but starting on the second string C, instead of the fifth string C. I'll even tell you that the high note is on the fifth fret of string one." ●

"I'm disgraced," I had to admit when I'd fumbled my way through it, playing every wrong note there is.

"You're not disgraced! You're starting to learn! You start simple and work your way up. The ears can be trained, and 'playing by ear' is a most constructive way to begin. It is all worthwhile because to know the sound of the notes is to make the guitar your own singing voice, and thus an extension of your emotional life!"

xi. *The Shape of Things to Come*

"What shall I study at home?" I inquired when don Diego indicated we'd reached the end of the lesson.

"Well, I wasn't prepared for this, you know. Let me think . . . ah yes, two things. One, I want you to come up with ten tunes or so that you can play by ear on the C scale."

"Ten?!"

"Five?"

"Three?"

"Whatever you can manage. Go back into your memory—Christmas carols, popular songs, lullabies . . ."

"Jingles?"

"I don't know any of those, but OK. Second, I want you to learn to play the C scale up and down in eighth notes using dedillo picking. I will write a couple of exercises.

a.

b.

"I think that's enough," he said when he finished writing.

But I did not think it was enough.

"No new music, don Diego?"

"New music? You expect new music?! You show up without a moment's notice and expect me to produce original compositions for you just like that?" He snapped his fingers.

"Uh, any old music will do. Maybe you have an old guitar manual I can . . ."

"New music, eh? I rather like the idea. *You* have put a challenge to *me*, Alfonso! Very good, and you wanted to know something about the Third Realm, too, eh?

"Oh, for sure!"

"OK, we'll let the composition go half the distance to the Third Realm, as it is my policy never to let an apprentice get his head in one realm while his feet are still in the realm before. He'll stumble, every time."

Don Diego shut his eyes and rubbed his chin. "Hmm, what did you say your girl friend's name was?"

"Melinda."

"Me-LEEN-da, Meleenda—and her last name?"

"Vossinovsky."

"I'll stick with Melinda. Now give me a moment to think."

Again he shut his eyes. This time his concentration seemed much deeper. It was strange to think of the silence in the room in contrast to the sounds seething in don Diego's brain. He began to write and sing,

Me-leen-da   Me-leen-da

Me-leen-da, Me-leen-da. "Melinda's Tune" was soon complete, and in a moment, the accompaniment too had been penned.

MELINDA'S TUNE

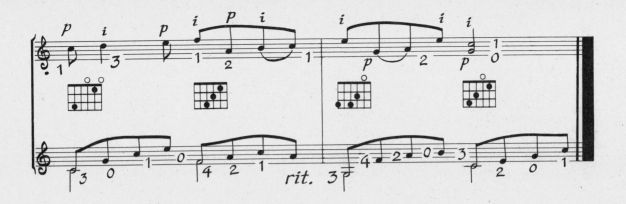

"I don't know anyone at school who can play this with me, don Diego."

"You have your tape recorder here?"

"Yes."

"Well, get it out, get it out. I will record both of these for you. Then you can take turns playing accompaniment against melody and melody against accompaniment."

I looked for contrasts in the new tune.

"I see a few differences, don Diego. This piece is in eighth notes, and none of today's melodies have been in eighths."

"That's true, but it has nothing to do with the Third Realm. It's more a test of your dedillo picking skill."

"How about the accompaniment? Does that have something to do with it?"

"Yes, you're warm."

"How about the flatted note in bar six?"

"Warm again."

"Where is A flat?"

"Same place as G sharp."

"Where is G sharp then?!"

"The first fret of the third string."

"But *why* are there two names for the same note? That's illogical, if not ridiculous."

"Ridiculous, eh? Well, you'll see—knowledge of sharps and flats is part of filling the Five Lesser Gaps."

"The Five *Lesser* Gaps?"

"A matter of the Third Realm."

"Then are we at an impasse?"

"Only until next week."

xii. *An Expulsion from Paradise*

Don Diego again saw me to the gate. Oddly enough, considering the dream, I was less apprehensive about jaguars than ever—the cry-wolf-effect, I believe. But I refrained from mentioning the nightmare to de Luna as I didn't want him to know that his hypothetical jaguar had gotten under my skin in any way, shape, or form.

Hoping to satisfy my curiosity about the estate I asked him if he would show me the garden grounds some time.

"That would be difficult, difficult. No, I can't do it."

"Why?"

"The master chose this spot for its seclusion, Alfonso. He has a passion for privacy."

"How about if we go sometime when he's not there?"

"That's . . . not possible. That is to say, one is never sure when he might not just drop in out of the sky. He uses a private plane to travel to and from here, you see."

"I take it that he is not just rich, but filthy rich."

"Even that, I think, is an understatement. No one knows the actual extent of his wealth."

"Wow, one of those," I said appreciatively.

"Does it sound good to you, Alfonso?"

"Sounds attractive, sure."

"You wouldn't want to be him."

"No, why not? I can see nothing wrong with it."

"That's how it looks from a distance, Alfonso. But I have observed the master up close, over a long period of time. His wealth has had bad effects."

"Like what?"

"His view of humanity is distorted. First there is the daily compromise of morality necessary to amass such a mountain of lucre. It teaches you the fine art of being a bastard, all right. And second, everyone could be out to get you, your friends, your numerous competitors and outright enemies—who is sincere? Who can he trust? He's become as nasty as an old bear with ticks in his hide."

"Aw, don Diego, he probably started out mistrusting everyone, anyway."

"Maybe so. He's had three wives. I think he trusted them, and then they skinned him alive in court! He keeps a lot of pets now and talks to them as though they were human."

"Well, there's a soft streak in him then."

"Let me tell you about one of them—the watchpig."

"Watchpig?!"

"Yes sir. He's an evil-tempered, battle-scarred, 300-pound wall of charging lard—blind as a bat. He'll ram anything that makes a sound he doesn't recognize, and sometimes things he does recognize, like me."

"What do you do then?!"

"What do you think keeps me in shape, Alfonso? I run! If I was really in dire straits though, I'd pitch a rock in the direction of the nearest wall. The watchpig rams the wall at full tilt, and after that he usually forgets what he's doing for a while. Poor old guy is getting punchy, taking on so many walls, trees, and cars. Doesn't do much for his face either, but then it never was too pretty, anyway."

"Your boss is beginning to sound rather eccentric."

"He is. That's another bad effect of the money. First it isolates him, then it allows him to indulge his whims and strange notions to the hilt."

"Tell me more about him—about these eccentricities of his."

"Well, about ten years ago he became obsessed with the thought of growing old and dying. After consulting all the best doctors, he came away assured that no matter what he did, it was going to happen to him, and there was no escaping it. At that point he decided to go to

India to seek the answers he needed. He was gone one month, and when he returned he had a half-dozen bearded gurus with him. Defending his fortune was a full-time occupation, you see, so rather than stay in India for years studying the various schools, he brought a chunk of India back to Venezuela with him, where he could dissect it at leisure."

"So they all moved in here? Six gurus?"

"Six gurus. Later, their aunts and uncles, their students, and their families. The master set them up in Caracas in apartment buildings he owned. There was a lot of trafficking back and forth, of course, and for that purpose he bought them cars, big shiny cars. And he gave them credit cards too, for gas and food, and western clothes."

"Didn't he realize he was being taken advantage of?"

"For some reason his instincts completely failed him. I wondered why. Well, it seems to me now he was filled with a new-found love of mankind. He was going to make this place the center for the spiritual development of the Americas. It was possible world enlightenment was going to begin to dawn here, right here."

"I should think you would have been excited about the spiritual center, too, don Diego."

"The boss should have listened to me, Alfonso, I could have told him what was going on. I was excited at first, too, yes. Then I talked to some of the gringos . . ."

"What gringos?"

"The ones camping in the gardens. Some of them spoke Spanish. When they told me they had given their savings to the gurus, I knew something was wrong. I would never exchange money for the Three Realms, nor would I take an apprentice just because he could pay the price tag, but they did, so it seemed fishy to me, and I kept my distance. What's more, I soon got the distinct impression that the young people's vision of Paradise did not include a poor, cockeyed, grubby old gardener who did not even speak English.

"If only the boss had listened to me, you know, none of it would have happened. I saw all the classic signs of disease."

"What signs?"

"A group that pretends it doesn't have a pecking order, when it has one that gets into every corner of a person's life; people obliterating themselves in the group and calling that self-discovery—the whole thing was bound to become corrupt, and it did."

"What happened?"

"Now to me the self is discovered through great loneliness, a loneliness which matures into the art of self-sufficiency. But on the other hand, this must be tempered by a lot of bumping around in the real world, too. And this world of the master's was unreal. They sat around staring at their navels all the time—reminded me of praying, and fat lot of good prayer did to improve my father."

"How did things come out, then?"

"Let me say this, it's a pity when self-discovery is achieved without a means to express it. That is the purpose of teaching the Three Realms of Guitar Knowledge, so that these discoveries are not made in vain."

"But what happened?!"

"What happened?"

"To the spiritual center!"

"I was coming to that. Ten years ago, that's when it all ended—overnight, like that! Now here's an anecdote for you. The master was away on a business trip in Brazil when he got a financial report that caused him to rush back here. He arrived unexpectedly and witnessed some strange goings-on that he could not square with the spiritual aims of the foundation."

"Like what?"

"Bizarre things, strange things."

"Tantric yoga?"

"Tantric yoga? Does that include gringos swinging from the chandeliers and running around naked? Ordering altars of flowers for the gurus' daily sermons, to be flown in at incredible expense?!"

"Wow."

"Some sort of party had been going on for three days, and there was a lot of damage to the house, too."

"An orgy, eh?"

"Hmmpf."

"What happened when he saw what was going on? Did he blow up?"

"No, he stayed out of sight, then he came and got me and we went into town. I gave him the complete lowdown on what had been going on, and he made certain arrangements over the phone. In the early morning we came back and waited at the airstrip. Precisely at dawn three planes came in and unloaded a squad of about twenty men in jumpsuits. Fortunes of the caliber of the master's always employ a number of such troops."

"Don't tell me they . . . ?"

"Oh no, no—they didn't even have guns. They just quietly and peaceably went into the house and herded everybody out. They were most polite about hurrying the people along.

"So, out they came, the gurus and the students, dressed in bathrobes, or with just a sheet pulled around them, some barefoot, some with slippers. The master assembled them in a group and made them stand at attention. But I think some of those poor people didn't even wake up until he started shouting at them."

"Didn't anyone speak up at all?"

"Yes they did, but when he ordered them to be quiet, believe me, they were quiet."

"First, he pulled some papers out of his coat pocket and began reading. It was his financial report. He started by calmly reciting the list of expenses since the beginning of the dream, but by the end he was livid and losing control. 'Six million dollars! SIX MILLION DOLLARS!' he shrieked. See what money does to you, Alfonso? It upsets you with its comings and goings.

"Then he began to list their sins, depravities, and extravagances. He paced up and down, waving his arms, shaking his finger—not noticing he had lapsed completely into Spanish! The speech then spread out to include a denunciation of greed and corruption and vice in all forms, in religion, in politics, government, art, law—and even business. I thought the veins in his head were going to pop before he finished. But at last he threw the papers to the ground and marched back to the door of the house, where he turned and waved his hand before entering.

"At that signal, the goons ushered everyone—dressed just as they were—toward the waiting planes. And yes, there was protesting then. But it availed them nothing—for that's how they left, barefoot, wrapped in bathrobes and bedsheets. In two weeks he had cleared out every last vestige of them."

"A sad ending for a spiritual center."

"I think it was the end of the master's last dream. After that he became more cranky, cynical and suspicious than ever. He fired all the help at the estate except me. Then he had the road from the estate into town torn up and obliterated. He ordered me to let all the footpaths go to seed too, and not to repair or maintain the wall that fronts the street. The results you see."

"No wonder I nearly got lost on my way up here the first time."

"It's a miracle you found the cabin at all."

"Where is the estate, I mean, in relation to your place?"

"Oh, Alfonso, I wouldn't want to tell you. What need do you have of knowing anyway? Why arm your curiosity, eh? The master welcomes no visitors, I tell you. He no longer even talks to me except to bark an order, and I think it would jeopardize my job merely to suggest bringing in one of my friends to trespass upon his kingdom."

So my desire to see the estate was decisively squelched, at least for the while. At the stone gate we agreed to meet at 2 P.M. the following Saturday and shook hands.

'Elated' is the best word to describe my mood on the drive home. I had struck a compromise between the two worlds where I desired knowledge and power, and positive developments were taking place in both. I had finished the Second Realm of Guitar Knowledge and I had the Third Realm to look forward to, and at school I had turned in an outstanding midterm report, as well as volunteered to deliver a special lecture sure to repair my reputation with Dr. Forzosa.

Everything looked splendid indeed.

xiii. Postscript by Dr. Felix Forzosa

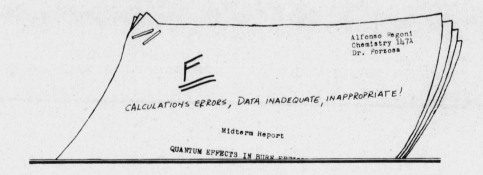

PART THREE

●

THE THIRD REALM
OF GUITAR KNOWLEDGE

LESSON V:

Passport to the Third Realm

i. *A Reluctant Acolyte*

The staccato rhythm of tennis shoes thumping against cobblestones in double time, the urgent rushing of air through searing bronchial tubes, the rattling of a guitar against the walls of its case as it jogs awkwardly against flexing, thrusting legs.

These were my sensations as I ran up the narrow street toward the top of the hill. I could feel the papers and books under my left arm squirming closer to freedom with every stride. Suddenly they slipped loose and all but the two end pieces tumbled to the ground. A helpless feeling came over me as I watched the breeze tease the corners of the loose papers, then send them flipping and sliding in a dozen different directions.

I set the guitar down and as it fell over on its side I began chasing the errant sheets all over the street.

I had been racing to meet don Diego at the estate entrance, and I was late—an hour late for our two o'clock appointment. How had I let it happen when I had in fact arrived two hours early, at noon? If only I hadn't stayed up all night the night before, I undoubtedly would not have made such a gross error.

Coming into town I had gone directly to a café with my books and, plying myself with cup after cup of syrupy, thick Venezuelan coffee, had done some serious and productive studying. I remembered looking at my watch at 1:30—somehow the next time I looked it had been 2:50. It was as if I had been in a trance. When I had realized how late it was I had run out of the café and taken the shortcut to La Cuesta, the highest street in town, on foot. The wall in front of the estate ran along the far side of La Cuesta Street.

All this fanatical devotion to studying wasn't born out of some masochistic streak, it was all in the name of survival. After the unbelievable failing mark on the midterm lab report, the lecture I was to give Monday had assumed a new and crucial significance.

In fact, considering the gravity of the situation, I felt it was a major concession to be coming to don Diego's at all. But then, I couldn't very well flake off on the heels of that impassioned speech which had won back my apprenticeship.

As I hopped along, stooping down, the devilish papers seemed to dodge away from my fingers like skittish stray chickens. How extreme had been the swing of the pendulum in one short week!

Dr. Forzosa simply refused to even discuss the failing mark with me. He said either I should be able to sort it out for myself or I didn't belong at the University; any error so obvious didn't need explanation; he was too busy to be giving courses in remedial undergraduate chemistry—I should ask a teaching assistant about it.

I began to have nightmares, and not about jaguars. Once I dreamt I was arrested and put on trial, only I didn't have any idea what for; another time that I had started a class and then completely forgotten about it until the day of the final exam, which I woke up late for anyway.

Naturally, I did take the paper to a teaching assistant, and in due course we found the error. But it didn't seem so obvious to me, nor to him, nor in retrospect did the grade seem just. But the T.A. said Forzosa was just testing my mettle and I could still pull a *B* for the course by doing well on the final.

Me, a *B?!*

Well, perhaps I would get an *A* on the final, and then again, perhaps I would not; my confidence had been completely undermined. But I did have one ace up my sleeve—the lecture I had elected to give Monday morning.

While in the States I had been fortunate enough to study a certain refining process discovered by Professor Wood, whom I mentioned in passing earlier. This process had been attracting a degree of attention in the literature recently, and I had volunteered to give an account of my experience and my understanding of the techniques. Since the subject matter was near to Forzosa's specialty, I had invited him and he had agreed to come. Here then was an outstanding opportunity to redeem my reputation with him. I was good, and I knew I was good—all I needed was a chance to show it. But I knew that every word I used in the lecture had to be supported by thorough background research if I was to field all questions, particularly those of Forzosa himself, for he was sure to indulge in his favorite sport—trapshooting the thinking of his students.

Therefore I had made an unstinting, all-out effort to prepare for my talk—but unfortunately I had given correspondingly little time to studying the guitar. In fact, I had played "Melinda's Tune" scarcely five times, if that. Thus, I was facing today's guitar lesson with fear and trepidation over what don Diego would think of my rusty playing —not to mention this very poor opening performance—showing up an hour late!

With the papers hastily bundled together, I resumed the uphill run. Shadows from the two- and three-story buildings on the narrow street were chilly as I made my way toward the patch of sunlight beyond the two sentinel buildings, one of them a church, at the top of the rise. Rounding the corner by the church steeple, I looked across the street and to the right, down the stone wall toward the gate—but there was no sign of don Diego.

The question now posed itself: Should I hike up the mountain alone and risk encountering the jaguar? The alternative was to turn around and go back home. I felt that that was out of the question, which left me with the former choice only, so I began putting one foot in front of the other toward the mountain and the forest.

The caffeine made me jumpy as I passed under the high domed ceiling of knotty branches and tangled foliage. "Hell," I swore, "if it weren't for this unicorn of a jaguar, I could look at this whole thing as if it were a harmless tropical terrarium." Instead, the emerald leaves, the gnarly vines threaded about tree trunk and branch, and the colonnades of light which beamed down from cracks and holes in the roofing of vegetation above all conspired to suggest that jaguar eyes lurked within every bush and jaguar paws trod this selfsame path every day.

I was relieved when at last don Diego's cabin appeared ahead, and I hurried through the weeds to the door. I knocked. No response, just a muffled echo. I knocked again and the door came slightly ajar. I leaned inside—dark, musty, stale cigar smoke.

"Don Diego?" I walked in, set my guitar case on the floor and dropped my books on the little table. I sat down and sighed heavily.

"Well, possibly he will show up," I thought. "At any rate, I need a rest."

But my mind was restless, so again I broke open the books and started scribbling on note paper.

Two hours elapsed and the sun was beginning to hang low; it was already behind the trees. It was time to go back; I could not delay another minute. I placed the note I had written to don Diego in the center of the table and went to the door. I pulled it open and drew back in alarm at the dark shadow which blocked the frame.

"Alfonso!" said Diego de Luna, evidently as shocked as I was.

"Don Diego, I missed you at the gate."

"Yes, our appointment was for two."

"I'm sorry."

"Quite all right, you're here now. May I come in?" A smile flashed across his face.

"Oh, excuse me," I said and backed away from the door.

"I've been up at the estate, catching up on some chores. Did you warm up?"

"Uh, a little."

"Good, good. Break open your case again, then, and let's get started."

"Yeah, but it's getting late. It's going to be dark soon."

"Pshaw! That's all right—why do you think I'm in a hurry, eh? I've got to go into town tonight myself. I've got an engagement at La Fortuna."

"An engagement? To play guitar?"

"Yes, you bet. I'll be glad to give you an escort to the bottom."

"But it's a long drive back."

"Well, whether you leave now or later, it will be a night drive, won't it? Say, Alfonso, is this all the enthusiasm you have for the Third Realm of Guitar Knowledge, which I remind you is the subject of today's lesson?"

"Oh no, it's not that, I guess I'm just tired. You're right, it won't make that much difference to stay awhile, and why come all this way for nothing? I'll stay."

"Have a seat then, I will get my guitar."

ii. Overview of the Third Realm

To my relief, rather than going into the home study I should have done, don Diego began immediately with the Third Realm of Guitar Knowledge. However, my exhaustion was by now so complete that it was only with the greatest difficulty that I could attend to his words.

"The Second Realm grew out of the First, Alfonso. How was it done?"

"How?" I blinked wearily.

"What was the refinement that expanded our powers of expression?"

"Oh, oh—in the First we strummed six strings, in the Second, selective strings."

"Correct. The Realms are separate, that is, they sound distinctive, but there are organic bonds between them. There are three such links between the Second and Third Realm, which I shall now describe.

"One, in the Second Realm we filled the Five Gaps, we learned the natural notes and we fixed them in our mind's eye as white, like the white keys of the piano. In the Third Realm we will learn the Five Lesser Gaps, which correspond to the five black keys of the piano. This will give us the freedom to play not just in the key of C, but in any key under the sun.

"Two, in the Second Realm we learned to play a melody line and we learned to play the chords as arpeggios. Now in the Third Realm we will learn to *blend* melody and chords."

"Ah, like Melinda's Tune, only as a solo."

"Right."

"I don't see how you can do that."

"It is quite possible—it is even possible to play two melodies at once. The whole idea was foreshadowed as soon as we separated the thumbstroke and fingerstroke. We made them into two independent lines, now we will increase the independence.

"This brings us to the third bridge between the two realms. To carry off the blending of melody and accompaniment convincingly, we will need a technically higher, more powerful form of fingerpicking."

"Super-picking."

"Do you have any questions?"

"Yes . . . where do we begin?"

iii. Finding Sharps and Flats

"We shall begin with the Five Lesser Gaps."

"Where are these five?"

Don Diego began sketching something.

"They're like black sheep standing in the herd of white natural notes. Here, let me darken their positions on this chart . . . now, please locate them on your guitar, using your index finger as a pointer." ●

"Then the Five Lesser Gaps are the sharps and flats, right?"

"That's right," he said. "Do you know what a sharp or a flat means to a guitarist?"

"Raise or lower a note?"

"By one fret! Don't forget that. A double sharp (×) means raise it *two* frets. A double flat (♭♭) means *lower* the natural note by two frets.

"Now perhaps that relieves the puzzlement you had about G♯ and A♭ last week, and how they could both stand for the same note."

"Well, I understand *how*, don Diego, but I'm no closer to understanding *why*."

"Why, eh?"

"There's no logical reason for it, is there?"

Don Diego shook his head.

"There are reasons, good ones. It has to do with the role of the notes. Let's take an F♯ for example."

"An F♯ it is."

"It so happens that the key of G major has one sharp in it."

"F♯, no doubt."

"Indeed so."

"But that doesn't explain anything—I mean, why not a G♭?"

"Why not indeed. You try it, recite the scale and substitute G♭ for F♯."

"G, A, B, C, D, E, G♭, . . . G. Hmm."

"See? Isn't that more confusing than the highly alphabetical, G, A, B, C, D, E, F♯, G! Eh?"

"I have to grant you that."

"I could give you an equally persuasive use for G♭ and many more examples, but have I made my point?"

"Well enough, I suppose."

"Speak up if you disagree."

"No, no, go on."

"Good, now let's learn these five new notes in detail. All of them are invaluable in learning to play music in other keys. And they will be quite easy to pick up if the natural notes are firmly fixed in your mind's eye—they are by now, aren't they?"

"Oh yeah, they're lit up in neon."

"Excellent! Because I want you to think of these five not as new notes, but as stretching the old notes, the naturals."

"Stretching?"

Don Diego raised his index finger.

"You see, *every* white natural note has a black note above it and below it, and named for it. So to find a sharp or flat, stretch the natural note up or down like elastic."

I shook my head.

"Take an A, for example. Whether you read an A♯ or an A♭, first see it as an A, that means second fret, third string, eh? Then the sharp or the flat will indicate the direction to stretch the basic A."

"You mean alter it up or down a fret?"

"Yes. Sharp: up a fret; flat: down a fret.

"Feeling the notes the way I suggest eases the confusion that arises when we think of sharps and flats as a whole new set of notes. What's more, it has applications I will show you later today . . . why do you look like that?"

"I'm thinking about F; F and E."

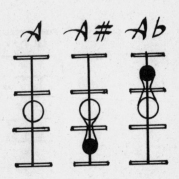

"Yes?"

"Well, F flat is the same as E natural. Is there a legitimate F♭ then?"

"Yes, F♭ is an alias for E natural, just as E♯ is an alias for F natural. Again, Alfonso, it is a matter of roles. F flats do occur when the need arises, and we do not call them E naturals."

"Hmm."

"We do call them *enharmonic equivalents*, however."

"In other words, enharmonic equivalents are notes of the same pitch but different names?"

"Precisely. Let's see how well you understand the general concept. Take this C . . . and draw a dark circle for C♯, please . . . and now one for C♭ . . . good. ●

"Now C♯ is the enharmonic equivalent of . . . ?"

"D♭?"

"Yes. And C♭ is the enharmonic equivalent of . . . ?"

"B♯?"

"Check your natural notes on the fretboard, please."

"Oh, B natural."

"Good."

"Don Diego, why are some of the natural notes, namely B and C, and E and F, just one fret apart, while the others are two frets?"

"A full explanation of that subject, Alfonso, belongs to the Second Domain of Guitar Knowledge."

"Is there any point in asking what that is?"

"Musical chemistry."

"A-ha!"

"But that is all I can say at this time. Let us summarize what we know about the accidentals now."

"The what?"

"These signs as a group are called accidentals. By the way, this is the sign for natural: ♮. It cancels the sharp or flat on a note, or just indicates that the note is natural when there may be some doubt. Look: (*See drawing at right.*)

"Good, not hard, eh? That's the principle to use when you read these notes. Find the natural, then go to the sharp or flat. ●

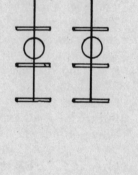

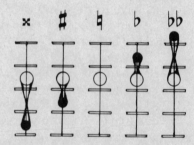

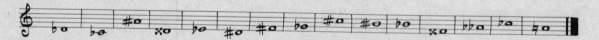

"This is the way the sharps and flats are laid out on the remaining strings. Notice that the sixth and the first strings are identical. Study this layout carefully while I write another reading exercise for you." ●

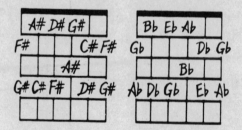

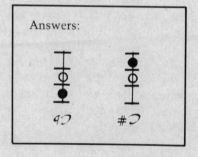

Holding my attention on the diagram proved to be difficult, my fatigue was becoming so overpowering. Several times I felt as if I was actually going to drop face down onto the table. Thoughts of the lecture on Monday kept intruding like a bad dream, until suddenly don Diego's voice cut through my reverie . . .

"I said, can you read these, Alfonso?"

"Huh? Oh yeah . . ."

"Then please, as you say their name, point to the natural and then go to the sharp or flat. ●

"Good, I congratulate you on passing a milestone. You can now identify all the notes up to the fifth fret. So, now let us apply this knowledge to unlocking the treasure trove of keys."

"How many keys are there?"

"Twenty-four, no less."

"Twenty-four?!"

"Twelve major and twelve minor."

"I never knew there were that many."

"It's not as bad as it sounds, Alfonso. Indeed, today we will look at only one new key, the key of G."

iv. One Key at a Time

"If the key of G has just one sharp, as you said, it's going to look a lot like the key of C, isn't it?"

"Only the F's will be different. We will use: one, natural notes as references; two, the G chord; and three, your common-sense notion of the 'right notes.' "

"My common sense?"

"Yes, the desire of your ear to hear the right note is sometimes the swiftest, surest way to grasp a new key. For example, play the natural notes from G to G . . . does this sound like a major scale?" ●

"No, it's not quite right."

"One note is wrong. See if you can find it—by ear."

My fatigue seemed to throw my hearing off. I fumbled through a few wrong notes.

"Start on the first string, third fret G and try to play the first eight notes of the Christmas carol 'Joy to the World,' eh? ●

"Excellent! Now try to play the same tune, starting down from the open third string G. ●

"Well done. In each case you had to raise the seventh tone of the scale from F♮ to F♯. In this way the seventh tone becomes a *leading tone*, so called because it is magnetically drawn toward G. B♮ is the leading tone in the key of C; the seventh tone in all major scales is called the *leading tone*. But your ear has shown us that you knew full well what the leading tone was before I told you about it. You now know the scale of G major, know it in the best senses, through your ears and hands. Now let me show you how I organize it in my mind, visually.

113

"First, since we are in the key of G, the G major chord expresses the fundamental harmony. So I think of that first:

"Then I think of the leading tones, the F ♯ 's that differ from the key of C:

"And to that I add the natural notes, which are the same as the key of C . . ."
"And which we know so well."
"Right, Alfonso.

"This equips me quite well to read music in the key of G. Please note that even though the key signature shows only one F ♯ , all F's will be sharped."

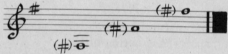

"What's a key signature?"
"Simply the group of sharps or flats at the beginning of each line of music. Don't worry about how they work for the moment. My intention is only to teach you the key of G. We can put off the lecture on musical chemistry until later."

I was grateful to be spared, for beyond a doubt any more lectures would have passed right through one ear and out the other at that moment.

"Play this for me, a simple test before we take on a new piece of music exemplifying the second dimension of the Third Realm." ●

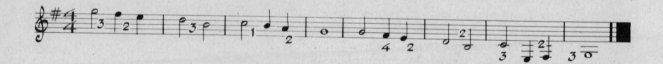

v. A Piece of the Third Realm

PARA CONSUELO

"What do you think of this, Alfonso? Last week a tune for a friend of yours, this week something for a friend of mine."

I was yawning too heavily to answer. Yawns are infectious, as they say, but don Diego seemed immune.

"Consuelo was a dancer I knew back when I lived in Caracas."

"Sorry," I said.

"Are you bored?"

"Bored? No, tired, that's all, like I said—tired."

"Uh-huh—well, this may perk you up. This piece marks your first crossing into the Third Realm, Alfonso. It is in another key, and it is melodious as well as chordal. Can you read it?"

My mind became shamefully blank when I stared at the page. As my unpracticed, unwarmed hands fumbled over the strings I felt like a drunk struggling to find his way through an unfamiliar room in the dark.

Don Diego was undeterred. He seemed to think the problem lay outside the obvious explanation, that I simply hadn't practiced.

"Obviously I underestimated the difficulty, but let's not give up. I believe you can manage it, yes, I'm sure of it. We'll just take it two bars at a time. We'll tear them down and build them up again!"

The following illustration shows how don Diego tore the piece down and built it up. Taking two bars at a time, the chord changes and fingerpicking pattern have been separated. After mastering each of these in turn, it should be relatively easy to combine them and perform the two bars. Next, the actual notes should be analyzed and performed.

Let the reader take the same route I did, and then discover how things went at don Diego's.

"Play it all the way through now, Alfonso," said don Diego at last. ●

My performance was not what one would call adroit.

"By the signs of all this slowing down and speeding up, you do not have your mind in the future and your hands in the present as you should. Think of it this way: You are in a boat on the ocean. There are four rolling waves coming your way, like the four bars of the first phrase. Every time you come to the crest of a wave you can see the remaining ones ahead of you. There is no difference in speed between them, their passage is very smooth and at equal intervals. Think of this as you play." ●

Even with the help of don Diego's fine analogy, I could not play any better.

"That's all right, Alfonso, it's to be expected when encountering something new on the guitar. I know you have persistence and a capacity for hard work. By next time you will have it—you always do prepare your homework magnificently. What was your homework for this time? The eighth-note scales, wasn't it? Ah, wonderful, you'll have no trouble playing some of the other music I wrote for today. For example —this. Note the Mexican flavor.

MEXICO, MEXICO

My play was halting and inaccurate.

"Hr-rumpf. Well, once you get the limp *out* of it, then the flavor will get *into* it. Er, how did you fare with 'Melinda's Tune?'"

I shot a glance to the floor, thinking now was the time to clear the air. Unfortunately, my hesitation instantly catalyzed the doubts de Luna had been entertaining all along. He started up from his chair, spun around and walked away a few steps with his hands behind his back. He was puffing up a tempest on the cigar. Then he stopped and looked sideways, over his left shoulder.

"You didn't practice 'Melinda's Tune' last week, eh?"

"I'm sorry to say so, but no, I did not."

"You didn't practice a lick last week, did you, Alfonso?"

"Don Diego, I was about to explain to you—I couldn't practice last week. Not at all. But . . ."

"Alfonso," he interrupted, turning to face me, "I have been sitting here . . ." Don Diego stooped down and tamped out his cigar on the floor, then stood up, looked at the butt for signs of life, and absent-mindedly dropped it into his coat pocket, ". . . sitting here, listening to you play as you have, unable to believe that, after what you declared to my ears last week, your ineptitude could possibly be due to a lack of practicing!"

"I know, don Diego. I meant to, I really meant to, but . . ."

"But what?" he demanded, turning sideways. "Too much school-work?" He glanced at me to see if the suggestion was to go uncon-tested. I let it go. "You told me you had that under control, huh? Listen, Alfonso . . ."

Realizing by his tone I was going to be lectured whatever I said, and being far too low on energy to muster a defense, I propped my head on my hands and, with profound weariness, listened to the sermon.

"Alfonso, you are young. Young people seem to think there is time enough for everything. I have no doubt you merely postponed your practice this week, and by next week you will have caught up. Young people always think they can catch up or go in nine directions at once, because to them time seems to have no end. But when you get old, like me, your perspective changes—you begin to understand how precious little time there is in this life for the accomplishment of one's aims. I don't impose demands because I'm ornery, but because I see the length of this journey you are embarking upon. It is awesome. The greater the distance you cross, the greater the distance you discover there is yet to travel!

"Eventually you come to realize that never in a single lifetime can you possibly traverse the Universe of Guitar Knowledge. Why? Because it is your own bottomless soul you are searching.

"Don't mistake what I'm saying for the old saw about art being long and life being short. I am not talking about the long list of composers and textbooks you could never finish studying should you grow so old as a great land tortoise.

"I am talking about a certain feeling known to you and you alone. It is a kind of longing, a form of desire, springing from the roots of your heart. You feel it most after you play strongly. When you're done, it's there—a mixture of satisfaction in what you've accomplished, and a sense of incompleteness for what you know you left unaccomplished. For it seems that no matter how worthy or excellent your creation, you can still imagine something better, or something else you have yet to say and which you know must be said!

"This is because you and only you sense what an imperfect reflection the work is of its source, which is your soul. This feeling is forever a spur to you to work on harder and further. It is the very oil that fueled the midnight lamps by which all the great composers honored in those textbooks wrote themselves blind, Alfonso. It is what gives meaning to the daily practice of scales and technical exercises, the endless polishing, polishing, polishing we do that gives people the idea we musicians are slightly mad.

"Because—what level of mental and physical culture is sufficient to translate visions of the spirit into musical language? Why, what limit could we ascribe, when we pin no limits on the complexity and depth of the soul, or the infinite variety of music?!

"That is why your wasted week disturbs me. You are young, you think you have all the time in the world. But I look at life from the far end, I know there is never time enough.

"Incidentally, I don't consider it a *bad* thing that you think this way—what else would give you young people the impertinence necessary to accomplish impossible deeds? But you must *examine* your thinking. The question is not whether you are too busy—the question is how badly do you want to make the guitar a part of you? If you want it badly enough, there is always room for guitar playing. You could take your guitar to school, perhaps, and practice between classes—I don't know what you'd do—but you'd find a way! Do you think I have never worked at anything in my life but playing the guitar? I understand how hard it is. There were many times I worked a job to put bread on the table, and feed my wife and children. And when I got home, my legs were often so tired they would hardly hold me up. But the need of my spirit was so strong I willed myself to tune the strings and play into the night. And when I woke up in the morning, if there were fifteen minutes to spare, I gave it to the guitar.

"Few people see any sense in this kind of behavior. . . . Let me tell you a story.

"I was sitting in my basement apartment in Caracas many years ago—I think I must have been about your age—and concertizing to the usual audience of cockroaches, when my girl friend showed up at the door. Whether I had invited her or not, I can't recall. Anyway, I let her in, gave her a warm embrace and a few kisses, and then I sat down and started playing the scales again. I had a few left to finish up, you see. She walked on around me and lay down on my bed—a mattress on the floor. She sighed once, and then was quiet, so I thought she was resting comfortably. But moments later, she was walking back in the other direction, to the door. So I said, 'Where are you going?' 'To get myself a sandwich,' she said. 'Can you pick one up for me, too?' 'Baloney?' she said. 'Fine,' said I. So she smiled her sensational smile and, flipping her hair over her shoulder, she shut the door. I went back to my scales. Alfonso, do you know, she never brought back that baloney sandwich? Now what do you think of that, my friend? Alfonso? . . . Alfonso?"

It was necessary for don Diego to repeat the latter half of this speech at another time, for while he was speaking I had fallen fast asleep.

vi. Trapped!

The thought came to me that don Diego had been quiet for a long time. My eyes blinked open and I found my head resting on my crossed hands on top of the table.

I sat up. A blanket had been draped over my shoulders and the cabin was dark. I felt for the matches on the cabinet, found them and lit one. It was 8:30. Obviously don Diego had left while I was napping —and now what? With no flashlight, and a mile of jungle between me and the road, I was stuck and I knew it. Even if I'd had a light, there was the jaguar to consider, or maybe the bandits don Diego claimed roamed the woods.

I went to the window. Cupping my hands over my eyes I put my nose against the pane. The forest was black as pitch, even though the sky was liberally dusted with brilliant, twinkling stars.

"How long will I have to wait here?" I wondered. I began to fret over the complications that would be caused by having to spend the night. I had to be in tip-top shape for the lecture Monday, but looking at don Diego's short, narrow cot, the prospects for a good night's sleep seemed rather dim.

By two A.M. my guitar mentor still had not returned. I was sitting at the small table over which I had spread my books and papers. The kerosene lamp was providing the light, and I had found biscuits to go with the tea I had brewed. The biscuits were about five inches across, tender as the average leather shoe sole, and as tasty as sawdust, but they were better than nothing, which was the second item on the menu.

I dropped my pencil. It was impossible to concentrate anymore. Even though the tea was keeping me half awake, it was time to give up on don Diego and try to go to sleep.

I lifted the lantern and went over to the bed. Immediately two mice, or maybe three, scuttled for cover underneath and out to the darker corners of the room. My heart was still pounding when I pulled back the blanket on the bed and discovered an enormous black beetle with caliper jaws sitting on the border of the mattress. He began to crawl toward the crack between the bed and the wall, but before he could get away I had swept him into my guitar case and tossed him out the open door. His body thudded softly when it hit the ground, and I could hear him picking his way through the grass. But then I noticed many other more eerie sounds coming from beyond the reach of the lantern.

I hurried back inside and shut the door—no bolt. By now my peace of mind was hopelessly shattered. I went back to studying as a means of escape, but now the smallest noise instantly suggested the scaly belly of a snake gliding over the floor, the velvet tread of a tropical spider, or the claws of some hideous nocturnal monster digging into the cracks around the door.

Sleep was impossible. I passed the rest of the night in this condition—under the spell of my own fears, almost afraid to move from the table.

I blamed don Diego for my predicament. Why hadn't he wakened me? If he had, I'd be back in Caracas. Now I'd be spending half the next day driving home. And so my thoughts went, around and around in circles.

When the sun finally began to tint the sky a shade of violet I felt compelled to go outside and deal with the consequences of my tea-drinking.

Out there, though, the world was peaceful and calm, and the air was fresh, and when I came back inside, the spell seemed to have been broken. My forehead became cool, my limbs grew heavy, and my eyelids felt weighted.

It was the birds beginning to twitter that finally relaxed me completely. I took the lamp over to the bed and checked between the covers—all clear. I lay down and turned the knob until the flame died.

I was beginning to drift off when the volume of the bird chatter began to increase to phenomenal proportions. It was the normal sort of party birds hold at dawn, but much more intense than anything I had ever heard back home. (But then, trees are scarce in my part of Los Angeles, and parrots even scarcer.)

I rolled over and covered my ears. I formed a wish. I wished hard that the mist I'd seen up on the mountain the other day would flow down a little farther and blanket the forest, chilling the birds back to sleep for another hour—or two. I pictured it happening, peaceful gray hordes pouring through the branches, skimming over the ground, filling up the hollows and inundating the knolls. The image grew stronger, the world quieter, and I began to smile. I seemed to feel a cold draft on my cheek, and as I opened my eyes slightly, I thought the gray mist was really there, coasting past the window, testing the seams around the frame with cool, gray fingers.

Then, remarkably, streaks of gray began to seep in through the cracks in the walls and the floor and spiral in the void at the center of the darkened room. The growing pinwheel rotated slowly, like a galaxy in space, assuming solidity. At last it formed a roiling mound of opaque clouds as high as the ceiling, and then the center of the vortex drew back like a burrowing worm leaving behind a cave with walls of slowly churning fog.

This quiet cave looked very tempting to me. But what happened next is a tale I had occasion to tell to don Diego not long after, and so I shall withhold it for now, seeing a better time for its unraveling further ahead.

vii. A Case of Intoxication

When I awoke it was to the sound of don Diego's snores. He was there in the room, asleep in a chair. The chair was tilted against the wall, and his guitar was propped by his side. He had on a wide-brimmed hat, pulled down over his face to block the sunlight that streamed through the windows. His legs were crossed and propped up on the table.

When I said his name he answered me with a fusillade of snores. The whole scene was very amusing, and I walked out of the cabin before starting to laugh out loud. Evidently he had returned while I was asleep, but had gone to sleep himself before even getting around to waking me up. Perhaps he was a victim of his own guitar. But there was more that was amusing me—something inside, something planted by my dream. I took some deep breaths. The fresh air was exhilarating. Though by my watch I'd had a scant four hours of rest, I felt like beating my chest like Tarzan and running in circles. So I did.

Then I collapsed in the grass and stared up at the sky with a rapturous smile on my face. Anyone would have thought I'd become slightly unhinged by stress and lack of sleep. I sat up and looked at the mountain ridge—no mist—there never had been. Everywhere the forest was rippling with a newly risen wind. Overhead some heavy clouds were mounting up. At this altitude they were carried by with uncanny speed, adding and annihilating substance, vigorously transforming themselves as they went. The weather was changing.

I jumped up from where I sat, crept back into the cabin, and stole away with don Diego's guitar. In the yard I turned the armchair and the footrest around to where I could face the mountains. I sat down to play, and I felt as though don Diego's guitar were a prism, shedding rainbows at a touch.

viii. A Classical Temptation

Some time later I heard the cabin door open and close and I stopped the strings. Would don Diego be mad, I wondered, because I'd taken his guitar without permission? I got off the chair and moved to the footrest just before don Diego turned the corner by the house, holding his hat and running his hand through his wild gray and white hair. As he adjusted his sunglasses on his nose he looked my way, tilted his head to the side to focus his eye, and then smiled and waved the hat at me.

"How do there, Alfonso?"
"Good morning, don Diego."

"So it was you made off with my guitar, eh?"

"Sorry, I just felt like playing a good guitar."

He walked up, glancing first at the roof, then at me. It was the length of the shadow he was sizing up.

"You haven't been playing out in the sun, have you?"

"Oh no."

"Then there's no problem. How are you?"

"Fine, never felt better." I was not about to lose face by complaining that some mice, a bedbug, and my own tea-drinking had kept me awake all night.

"That's good—I wondered," he said, sitting on the arm of the chair.

"Why?"

"Couldn't have waked you yesterday if I'd planted a stick of dynamite under your ass."

"You tried to wake me up?"

"Of course—but it was like trying to balance a sack of potatoes on a bottle of rum, trying to get you to sit up, let alone stand. I figured you were best off left alone."

"So that's why you left me here."

"Sí."

"I was pretty mad when I woke up, you know—I wanted to get home yesterday."

"Ha! In your condition you weren't fit to steer a burro, much less negotiate Camino Cielo [the highway down the mountain to the flats]. You would have jumped the road and gone down the short route, and then where would I have been?"

"You?! Ha!"

"Out one guitar apprentice, that's where—do you think they grow on trees, amigo?"

"Well, I suppose you did the right thing. But what about you? You must have been gone all night."

"Well," he drawled, scratching his bristly chin, "I guess I overdid the free drinks at the bar, Alfonso—I forgot how much it affects me. I had a fine old time, but I wasn't much good for mountain climbing when we were done—three A.M. or so, I think. Anyway, I got up early just so I could come back here and check on you. When I walked in, I found you snoozing and everything in order, so I thought I'd just play guitar to nudge you out of your slumber and get you going on your way in the right spirit. I detest alarm clocks, you know. . . . Here, hand me the guitar . . . thanks."

"Welcome."

"But," he said, strumming, "I only put the sand in my own eyes again."

"I guessed as much."

"What time is it, anyway?" he asked.

"Oh, 1:30—1:30! My gosh."

"What is it?"

"Oh, it's just a lot later than I thought." (Three hours—how had I played for three hours and not noticed?)

Don Diego strummed the guitar slowly and looked away at the mountain.

"Did you sleep well last night, Alfonso?"

"Oh, reasonably well."

"No nightmares this time?"

"None, well . . ."

"Hmm?"

"No, nothing."

"Nothing, eh? Guh-lad to hear it."

He began picking notes. They popped out with amazing clarity. He always seemed to play with twice the dynamic range I had. I was rather envious.

"A splendid day, don't you think?" he said.

"Yes it is."

"When the weather gets moody like this, Alfonso, I feel, I feel . . ."

He stopped playing and raised his hand, unable to find the words that matched his thoughts.

". . . like playing guitar, I guess," he said, and went back to strumming.

"When the weather's like this, there's a substantial increase in negative ion concentration in the atmosphere, don Diego. That's why you feel so . . . high."

He looked at me through his nearly opaque sunglasses as he went on playing and nodding his head.

"No, really, it makes it possible for your red corpuscles to hold more oxygen, and you get a rush from it, you see?"

"I knew I was feeling something, Alfonso. I didn't suspect it was 'negative ions.' Can you manufacture these things, these ions?"

"Sure, it's possible."

"So can I."

"Can you now?"

"Yes. This is 'Negative Ion Fantasia Number One.' Please listen . . ."

"Don't put me on."

"I'm not—I just made it up—out of my negative ions."

Don Diego began ripping up the fretboard, his left hand flicking through a blur of chord changes and scales so outrageously complex and difficult-looking, and yet so effortlessly executed, that I had to laugh out loud.

I shook my head. The piece was brief, but awe-inspiring.

"How . . . how the hell do you *do* that?"

"Stick around, maybe you'll find out."

"Sure! How long?"

"Twenty or thirty years, no more."

"Ha—I'll never find out, I'll never play like that."

"That's nothing to be concerned about. I keep telling you, not only will you never play like me, you don't want to. Don't be impressed by superficial things like speed. They're fun, but the only question, so far as I am concerned, is—can I hear Alfonso Fegoni, true to his muse, playing that melody? And that has next to nothing to do with speed, next to nothing whatsoever."

"How do you make the notes jump out like that—like they're popcorn in an open fry pan?"

"Ah, the finger technology of the Third Realm, that's how. Yesterday we discussed only two of the three dimensions in which the Third Realm enlarged on the Second. Can you remember them?"

"Quiz time already?"

"Come on, you've been up long enough."

"The Five Lesser Gaps, and the combination of melody and accompaniment."

"Correct. It remains to sophisticate your fingers so that the joining of melody and accompaniment can be truly consummated."

"Well, how does it work?"

"We need a power stroke that can bring the melody into relief over the other notes. Sometimes four strings are ringing at once—so which one are we to hear as most important?"

"Yeah, I follow."

"Up until now you have plucked the string with a semi-circular stroke, just as the bull paws the earth. This is called *tirando* (ti-RAHN-do), or *free stroke. Apoyando* (ah-po-YAHN-do), or *rest stroke,* is a more powerful technique. The finger goes in a straight line past the plucked string and lands on the next string up the ladder, burying its force there. Observe":

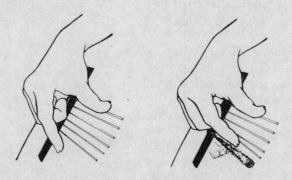

"You try," said don Diego and handed the guitar back to me. ●
The effort brought a few tantalizing successes.

"How long would it take to finish up yesterday's lesson, don Diego? I mean, showing me the third dimension of the Third Realm?"

"I see . . . our man of constant academic labor desires to know precisely how many minutes he will sacrifice to this guitar foolishness."

"Don Diego, I didn't mean it like that."

"Can't you tell when you're being ribbed, Alfonso? One hour, I should think, would be sufficient, at least to introduce you to the technique. Is that agreeable?"

"Sounds fine."

"Very well, let's go."

And with that we went into the cabin and began—

LESSON VI:

A Transformation

i. The New Brew

"I'm putting on some tea, Alfonso—do you want any?"

"Yes! Do you have any food to go with it?"

"Some biscuits."

"Oh."

"They're very good—made right in town with stone-ground flour."

"Stone ground, or ground stone," I muttered.

"How many?" don Diego said.

"I'll have one."

"One? You can have more, Alfonso—don't be over-polite."

"One will be fine."

"Very well."

I was monkeying with the apoyando stroke when don Diego set something down on the table. My eye caught the sparkle of it—a silver teapot.

"Gosh, what is this?"

"A beauty, no?"

"Yes, but where did you get such a thing?"

"Borrowed it from the estate house. It will never be missed. The master never has a need for such things any more."

"Is this because of a special occasion? It's not your birthday is it?"

"No, my birthday's not till April—but today *is* a special occasion, yes, indeed. It is the occasion of the transformation of a guitar player of the Second Realm into one of the Third Realm . . . you think I'm overplaying it?"

"Well, why not a little celebration?"

"Very good!" he said, standing at the side of the table and planting his hands on the wood with fingers spread. "Now, let's look at this silver object gracing the top of my humble table. What does it have in common with its predecessor?"

"A name, and that's about all."

"Teapot! They're both called teapots. Of course, as you have undoubtedly noted, the old one was a teapot, and this one is . . ." He lofted the silvery vessel above my head, ". . . a *Teapot!*"

"A-ha."

"Observe the exquisite lines, the filigree, the mirror-like polish; the quality of this craftsmanship is unsurpassed. Just look at the date on the bottom. Seventeen eighty-one, Alfonso. What would you call a teapot with a date like that on it, eh?"

"Old?"

"Old?! It is a *classic!* Such is the relationship between the Second Realm and the Third. The techniques of the Third are classical, they are of high craftsmanship."

"Classical guitar?"

"Something the matter with that?"

"I've always had trepidations about classical guitar, I guess."

"Why?"

"It sounds difficult and . . . aristocratic, sort of."

"Am I the aristocratic type?"

"Well, no."

"Darn right I'm not! What prejudice you show—didn't you do the apoyando stroke yourself just now?"

"I guess so."

"And as for the music, you can use the techniques to play whatever music you please! Expressiveness, that's what we're after, and I owe much of what I know to the classical players, including ones who have long since gone to join their Maker."

"Then you're not a classical guitarist?"

"No! Nor am I a folk guitarist, or a what-have-you guitarist, thank you. Guitar is just the medium, you see, de Luna is the messenger, and God knows the message! Tomorrow I may decide to play electric guitar, or maybe the violin—you never know. It depends on what one needs to say. Well, enough philosophy, Alfonso. Let's get in tune, eh?"

"Now the secrets of the Third Realm technique are hidden, not somewhere out there on that mountain, but right here under our very noses, on our fingertips, even in the way we sit."

"The way we sit?"

"It's a tin teapot way of sitting!"

"Oh."

"We shall learn another way. One that is simple and functional, yet elegant and noble. . . . You're thinking—what are you thinking?"

"You've been letting me sit wrong for weeks—why didn't you correct me?"

"I wouldn't show you anything *wrong.* No, no—just because it's tin doesn't mean it isn't good at serving tea. Do you think I act like I'm on the concert-hall stage playing serious solo guitar music when I play at the bar in town, eh? I sit just like that, casual, First Realm, Second Realm. If I had shown you this classical position a month ago you would have felt it was stuffy and hidebound. You've grown a need for it, it is useful to you now, so now's the time to learn it, eh?"

ii. *Classical Body Language*

"First uncross your legs and sit toward the front of the chair. Put this footstool under your left foot."

"How high is my foot supposed to be?"

"You wouldn't want it too high, not more than five or six inches. Now move your right foot back under your seat until the heel lifts about an inch, Alfonso. Back straight, please." (*top drawing*)

"Is my heel supposed to dangle over the ledge of the footstool, like yours?"

"Yes, that's why I prefer a level footrest. Both heels should feel springy, flexible, free to twist. If I sat flat-footed, like this . . . (*center*)

". . . I would be very stable, well-protected in case the earth should quake while I play, but frankly, though my playing is good, it is not known for bringing on earthquakes. Music flows and I want to be able to flow with it."

"Leaves your heel free to tap-tap-tap, too, I see."

"One does *not* tap-tap-tap in the Third Realm, Alfonso. That would be like . . . like belching in a library."

"Well, after all this tapping I've done I'm going to have a hard time giving it up, aren't I?"

"You don't give it up—you swallow it. Down it goes, and remains near your heart. You feel it, but now your body expresses the phrase, not the beat. Your face, your carriage, your hand and arm movements, all flow with the phrase. You'll see, it comes naturally.

"Now let's put the guitar into the picture."

He took his guitar, rested it with its shoulder curve on his left thigh, and the wider, hip curve on his right thigh. The upper edge of the guitar touched his chest, and a triangular open space could be seen between his body and the back of the guitar.

"Notice that the tuning gears are about shoulder high, Alfonso. Now as I complete the position . . . (*bottom drawing*)

"See if it does not give you a sense of being about to hear music with a certain amount of refinement and sophistication, serious music, that is. But does this mean humorless? Or 'aristocratic,' as you put it? No, don't be precious just because you are now adopting a classical pose. You must retain the vigor of the First and Second Realms!

"Now there are some practical improvements in this position, too. Notice the guitar touches my body only on the edges, so the sound projects to its full potential. Secondly, the guitar neck is stable, and if you will think a minute you will see a tremendous advantage in that."

"Freedom for the left hand?"

"Yes, it can fly all over the fretboard now; still you'd never get the sense that it was hard work to look at it, because the neck never need be jostled in the slightest. This stability is based on four points of support. Can you see them?"

"Right thigh, left thigh, chest, and right arm."

"Right arm! There's the main anchor. The weight of the arm falls fully on the hip of the guitar, pinning that side of the teeter-totter down and making the neck as steady as a flagpole. You must relax your right shoulder more, Alfonso."

"What part of the forearm actually rests on the guitar?"

"The most padded part, just in front of your elbow. Look, if you can swing your forearm freely and weightlessly, you probably have the right spot."

"When you do it, it looks like a well-balanced tone arm on a stereo turntable, don Diego."

"Ah yes, and when I touch the strings, the sound is like a miniature orchestra in itself—did you know Beethoven said exactly those words when he heard the playing of Mauro Giuliani?"

"Who was Mauro Giuliani?"

"Giuliani was a classical guitarist," don Diego winked; "take note of that.

"Now notice that the right hand hangs comfortably in front of the sound hole."

"What about the left arm?"

"Take hold of the neck, let your arm dangle, relax everything except your grip. That's it. With the arm relaxed and more or less in agreement with gravity, you can use it economically, just for what it was meant to do, helping the hand to dart from here to there like a hummingbird.

"By the way, the weight on the hip bones should be equal. You may have to turn your knees slightly to the left. But don't slump or twist your back. The muscles will get sore over a long practice session."

"That would be a good excuse for not practicing."

"Not for you, Alfonso, not unless you have a note from your mother."

"Ha-ha. You know, I'm having trouble getting my right hand to line up with the sound hole. Every time I fix one thing, something else gets out of whack."

Don Diego helped me seat the guitar correctly by pushing and pulling on it here and there, then he sat back and appraised his handiwork. I felt as if I were posing for a family portrait in a stiff new suit of clothes.

"When you get home try using a mirror to find a comfortable and esthetic position, bearing in mind what is functional. Each individual has a different body, so we learn to accommodate to the classical position in a personal way. If you understand and keep the four-point hold, then we have plenty to build on for now."

iii. Secrets of the Right Hand

Don Diego held up his right hand and turned it back and forth.

"Our next subject. This hand is vastly underestimated. People tend to be impressed by dexterity in the left hand without realizing the right hand is the heart of the performance.

"Why, it is as if we were to compliment the waiter instead of the chef on the fine cooking. The right hand is the chef, mixing recipes of tone color, balancing the volume across the strings and throughout the piece, and most of all expressing the rhythmic drive without which the music would be lifeless."

"But you can't play something if the left hand can't find the notes," I said.

"Oh yes, and the two must coordinate. But I have found most limitations and plateaus in a player's technical development can be traced to inadequacies of the right hand. Why, a player's whole personality—strong, weak, delicate, or tough and aggressive—can only come through the right hand."

"Guess so. Now that I think of it."

"And think of this, Alfonso—all the energy in the soul coming to the hand by decisions in the brain is ultimately transmitted across a thin sheath of nerveless horn at the tips of your fingers."

"I never thought of fingernails that way before."

"Indeed, but no other part of the finger is so intimately responsible for the sound, your sound, your personal guitar voice. So we must put first things first and take a good hard look at the nails."

Don Diego went fishing in his cabinet for a nail file.

"You know," he said, returning, "I think God wanted man to play guitar, because he gave us fingernails."

"What is the proper shape?"

"I will show you. In a moment you'll see why it is so useful.

"First, hold the file—a very fine abrasive file, not one that tears—with the sanding surface against the nail at right angles. Then gently sand the nail down until its contour matches the natural contour of your fingers. See? No longer than the horizon of the fingertips."

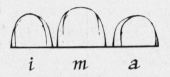

"Why use the file at right angles to the nail? Won't that make the edge fat and blunt?"

"You *want* it to be blunt. The thicker the nail, the richer the sound."

"Next, you smooth the nails with ultra-fine emery paper, and buff them up on a patch of smooth leather, or your blue jeans, if you wish.

"The final touch," said don Diego, rubbing his fingers on the side of his nose, "a serviceable lubricant—very inexpensive, too." ●

"I always played with my nails longer than this, don Diego. How am I going to pick the strings with nails this short?"

"You won't exactly pick the strings anymore, Alfonso. The edge of the nail, which we have so carefully polished smooth, forms a road. The escaping string rides slightly sideways across the road on its way to freedom. This makes for a tone like honey dripping from a tree branch.

"I really can't visualize what you mean—a road?"

"Here, I will show you."

Don Diego flashed out of the room and came back with some thick twine and a serving spoon.

"Hold this end," he said. He put his elbow on one corner of the table and I put mine on the other. We stretched the twine straight. "This represents a guitar string. This spoon represents your fingernail, see?"

"I see."

He put the concave side of the spoon flat against the string.

"You are accustomed to picking this way."

He drew the bowl across the string in a curving, tirando stroke.

"You get a sharp tone from this tip-of-the-nail type stroke, hence it is good for accentuating the metallic sounds near the bridge. The stroke we are going to learn now goes like this . . ."

He turned the spoon so that only the lower edge touched the string. This time he moved it straight across the string, that is to say, in a course parallel to the table top instead of curving up and away from it. The string bent in a V, and then the twine rode along the angled edge of the spoon blade and came free. (*See drawing.*)

Don Diego repeated this a few times slowly.

"You see, Alfonso?"

"I see!"

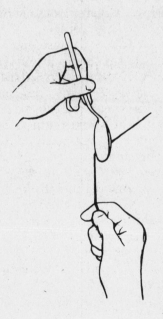

"Bear this in mind now as we set up the right hand to perform apoyando strokes.

"Sit in the classical position and shake your right hand awhile, until it feels rubbery and tingling—a quick, loose shake. ●

"Put your arm back in place and swing your wrist in to around four inches from the face of the guitar. Let your hand hang. Fine. Now rotate the wrist until your fingertips touch the strings. Don't lean the guitar back, please, just turn your wrist.

"Now we'll get a feeling for the end of the rest stroke, when the stroking finger hangs up on the support string."

"Working backward, don Diego?"

"Easiest way to unravel a maze, isn't it?"

"Right."

"Plant your index finger on string 2 and pull up. Now don't let the finger joint bend, keep it gently curved, but strong, firm. Good, exchange the middle for the index now, pull . . . good. Now the ring finger—pull . . . fine. ●

"Go back with each finger and once you put on the pull, try bouncing a little, testing the resilience of the string. Don't bob the wrist, use the finger muscles. ●

"Now, Alfonso, I want you to imagine a line joining the knuckles on the back of your hand. That line is now almost parallel to the strings."

"Is that good?"

"Yes, we do not want a handshake position."

"Do you want me to get my knuckles perfectly parallel?"

"Not necessarily. I don't want to see any tension anywhere. If you force the wrist into an odd angle, you slow down your strokes. Here, hold out your hand. Now keep clenching and unclenching your fist as you angle your wrist in different directions." ●

"Seems like it's easiest when the wrist is held perfectly straight."

"It's the natural way to move. Here, hold your fist over the sound hole and open your fingers gradually by relaxing. When they come apart just enough, put the thumb on string 6 and the fingers on 3, 2, and 1. Now line up the right side of the sound hole with the space between your middle and ring finger. This is called *home position*." ●

"Home position?"

"Home, because you always return to home. The finger movements are extensions of your energy, but there should be a constant memory of home position that keeps all movements as minimal as possible. The knuckles, for example, brush each other lightly and never spread apart into a spider hand. Neither does the hand bounce with the strokes (unless intentionally) because the power must be delivered consistently, deliberately, concisely. Concision is of the essence in this style. The hand works as a unit, almost as if the fingers were not separate at all."

"And the thumb, don Diego?"

"As before, the X is preserved, the thumb is held to the side. You want to be more careful about having it wiggle around when not in use, and there is a twist or two I will show you in a minute.

"Now let's look at the index finger. This is where the string contacts the nail, not at the tip, but near the corner where flesh and nail meet."

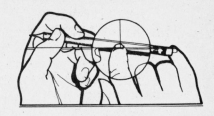

"Like the spoon?"

"Yes, yes. But the string touches the flesh *and* the nail. The sense of touch is important for expressive feeling. Here, take this pencil. Put it across the fingertip, like a file, forming a T. Tilt the left end of the pencil up . . ." ●

"Looks like about 20 degrees."

"Yes, now the string should go past your finger at an angle, like that."

"How do you make the angle?"

"I think we can best understand simply by doing it."

"Shoot then."

"Put the middle finger on string 2. Extend and poise the index finger over string 1. (As in illustration of rest stroke at beginning of this lesson.)

"Lower the index finger and find the right contact point with the string." *(See drawing at right.)* ●

"Like a woodsman about to split a rail."

"Good, now lift your 'axe' and cut down sharply and quickly through the first string, ending up with both fingers planted on the second string. ●

"Good, but don't let the index finger joints bend. No brushstrokes. Now repeat a few times, working for the best tone. Again, think of how the spoon represented the fingernail, try rolling your fingertips slightly counterclockwise by turning the palm. Hear the differences in tone color. ●

‸ = rest stroke

î-î-î-î-î-î-î-î-î-î-î-î-î-î-î

① --------------------------

"Try stroking with your middle finger now. Keep the index finger planted on the second string as you play." ●

m̂-m̂-m̂-m̂-m̂-m̂-m̂-m̂-m̂-m̂-m̂-m̂-m̂-m̂-m̂-m̂-m̂

① --

"Is this the next step, don Diego?"

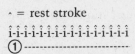

4 î-m̂-î-m̂|î-m̂-î-m̂|î-m̂-î-m̂|î-m̂-î-m̂|

① ---

"Very good. Double time now. Yes, your fingers are switching places quite neatly. ●

"Now reverse the accent. M-i-m-i will feel different than i-m-i-m because m will become the accented finger rather than i." ●

4 m̂-î-m̂-î|m̂-î-m̂-î|m̂-î-m̂-î|m̂-î-m̂-î|

① ---

A TRANSFORMATION

We then did each of the following patterns. It helps to tap a pattern before using it on the strings. ●

m̂-a-m̂-â   î-â-î-â   î-m̂-â-m̂   â-m̂-î-m̂
â-m̂-â-m̂   â-î-â-î   m̂-â-m̂-î

"There comes a time when we must change strings, Alfonso."
"You mean like this?" ●

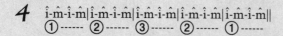

4 î-m̂-î-m̂|î-m̂-î-m̂|î-m̂-î-m̂|î-m̂-î-m̂|î-m̂-î-m̂||
　①------ ②------ ③------ ②------ ①------

"Yes, like that. But listen to your sound. There should be no difference in the volume as you change strings . . . you're doing well now.
Try each of the other finger patterns, too. ●

"Now when we go past the third string, you will not be able to
brace with your thumb."
"Why not?"
"The hand gets too far from home position, the fingers don't work
efficiently and the tone changes."
"What do you do with the thumb, then?"
"You let it dangle, but to the side. Here, keep this cigar held in the
crook of the hand, and the thumb will stay in the right place."
"Er, sorry. I hope you didn't intend to smoke that cigar." I picked
it up off the floor.
"I think people fail to realize, Alfonso, how a little dirt improves
the caliber of a cigar."
"I hate to think how you found that out. Darn—there it goes
again."
"I'll tell you what, if you improve the taste of that cigar any more,
I'll make an award of it to you, and we can both take a smoke break."
"Right now?"
"Right now."

î-m̂-î-m̂|î-m̂-î-m̂|î-m̂-î-m̂|î-m̂-î-m̂|î-m̂-î-m̂|î-m-i-m|
①------ ②------ ③------ ④------ ⑤------ ⑥------

î-m̂-î-m̂|î-m̂-î-m̂|î-m̂-î-m̂|î-m̂-î-m̂|î-m̂-î-m̂||
⑤------ ④------ ③------ ②------ ①------

"Well, Alfonso, you failed to improve the cigar at all. I will have
to withdraw my offer."
"Rats." I snapped my finger.
"So much the worse for you, my friend, but I am a man of my
word. Careful about your wrist now—even when you play on string 6,
it has got to be a good two to four inches away from the face of the
guitar, not leaning against it." ●

"This gives you the basic idea behind the right hand, Alfonso, let's consider the left."

"The classical left."

"Yes."

"Is there anything like home position for the left hand?"

Don Diego didn't answer, he just got up and went into the kitchen. He came back with a broom.

"Hold your left hand palm up and right hand palm down—now take hold of the broom handle, rifles ready."

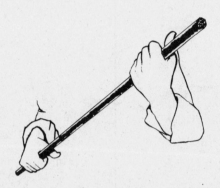

"Or guitars, right?"

"That's the idea. Overall, home position is like holding a pipe in your hands."

"In other words, the movement of the left hand relates to a closed fist, too?"

"This becomes more apparent as the pieces get more difficult. Sometimes the hand stretches, squeezes, or shifts, and then it has to recover, like elastic, to home position. On a long shift, for example, the thumb often lags behind, like so . . . when it should remain opposite the index or middle finger, like so . . .

"Put your left hand on the table top, Alfonso—palm down and fingers half-curled."

Don Diego rested his fingers on mine.

"Try raising your fingers, one at a time."

"Not easy, when you're holding them down."

"That's the point—you should always feel such resistance to leaving the zone of space just over the tops of the strings, unless it is deliberate, an expressive flourish.

"The next exercise combines the right and left hand. It will therefore test your timing and coordination. Let's do a dry run first.

"Put your right hand on top of the table and your left hand palm up underneath the table. As you tap the table with the i–m–i–m pattern in the right hand, simultaneously tap it with the 1–2–3–4 pattern in the left hand. ●

"Good, now pick up your guitar and play the same thing on the first string. The high frets are closer together, why don't you play on those? ●

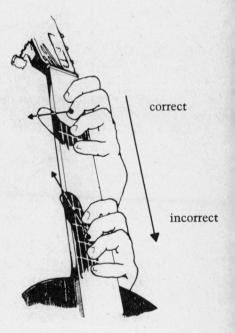

correct

incorrect

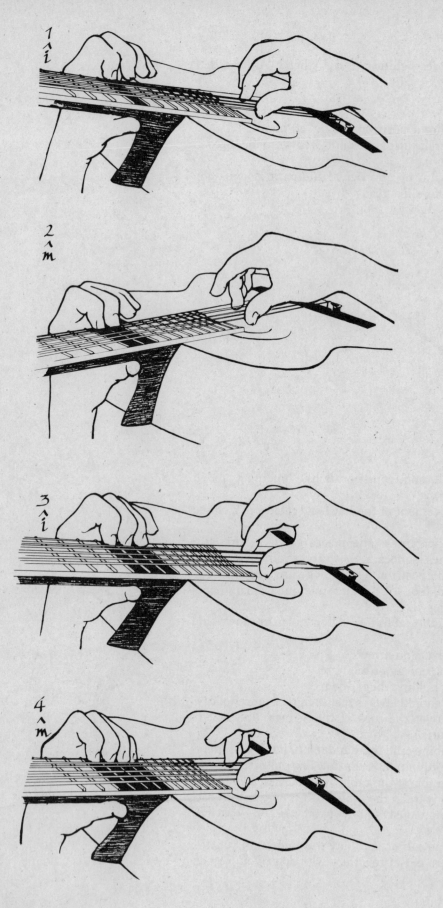

"Try sliding your hand progressively down the neck. See if you can keep all four fingers down on the first four frets, F through Ab. ●

"Fine, now reverse the pattern, lift the fingers, 4–3–2–1, while you play i–m–i–m. ●

"Funny how it's confusing me to reverse the pattern."

"Try reversing the right hand pattern—1–2–3–4, m–i–m–i." ●

"Wow, that gives me trouble, too."

"There are 24 possible combinations of left-hand finger movements, Alfonso.* They make excellent material for developing your finger independence, dexterity, preparing and holding skills, concision, strength, and so on. For example, any pattern can be made into a slur exercise. You could do a selection of the patterns every day and develop equal strength in all your fingers, particularly the weak fourth finger."

"For example?"

"1–2–3–4, for example. ●

"That was a hammer-on pattern. Here's a pull-off pattern. Be economical, now—don't use your wrist in a pull-off; make the fingers do the work. The hand must stay stable. ●

"Good."

"How do I practice it though? Not just on one string, do I?"

"No, by moving from string to string. Let's do that now with our simplest pattern. No slur as yet. And you can remain at the higher frets if that's more comfortable. ●

```
1-2-3-4 1-2-3-4 1-2-3-4 1-2-3-4 1-2-3-4
î-m̂-î-m̂|î-m̂-î-m̂|î-m̂-î-m̂|î-m̂-î-m̂|î-m̂-î-m̂||
①------ ②------ ③------ ②------ ①------
```

"Do it with two slurs, please." ●

```
⌒  ⌒   ⌒  ⌒
1 2 3 4 1 2 3 4 |
î    m̂   î    m̂   | (same picking pattern on each string)
①------------------------ ②------- ③------- ④------- ⑤------- ⑥ → ①
```

"Now try stepping up to the sixth string and back down, four strokes on each string and no slurs. Go slowly, we're not holding races yet. ●

"Now with the two-slur pattern again, please." ●

"Whew, are my fingers getting tired."

* See Appendix B.

"Shake your hand loose. Keep doing that from time to time—flex and stretch your fingers. Now, while you rest your hand, let me suggest a way you can improve your sound.

"When playing 1–2–3–4 there is a moment at 4 when the first finger reaches toward the next string. Unconsciously, 4 tends to give up its pressure, thus creating an unintended rest. You can smooth the connection by maintaining pressure on 4 while reaching with 1, the index finger. (*See drawing at right.*)

"The other 23 finger combinations give similar problems for all the fingers."

v. Putting It All Together

"Can you name some practical applications of this skill?"

"I'll show you some. All scales involve finger movements like these—so let's try playing the C scale with classical technique now. First, we'll study the right hand . . . ●

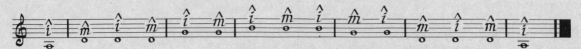

"Good, now the combination of both hands should be easy." ●

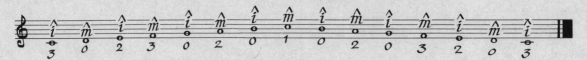

"What are the rules for right-hand fingering?"

"Fingering is an art in itself, which is to say, there may be more than one right way to handle a problem. But here's one rule: Never repeat a finger—never! You will not see i–i–i, or m–m–m, or a–a on a guitar score; it's just not done, not unless there's a special reason for it.

"Here, see how you handle this . . ." ●

"Wow, you'd think I could keep a finger from repeating if I put my mind to it."

"It's something that has to go beyond the mind. You must altogether free your mind of the decision process."

"How can I do that?"

"Put it in your fingers."

"In my fingers?"

"With the 24 patterns for the left hand."

"How?"

"Ten minutes a day, take ten minutes a day to play them across the strings with various right hand patterns. After that, you'll have no more problems."

"After what? How long?"

"A year or so."

"A year!"

"Don't think about that, Alfonso. Just think about doing the next ten minutes of practice well. And if you do it well, give yourself a pat on the back. Then do another ten and another. Don't make the mistake I made. When I started I thought I had a 50-year task ahead of me— just look what happened—a face full of wrinkles. Why, carrying the weight of that assignment turned me into an old man! Now let that be a lesson to you."

vi. *Looking Ahead*

"So far I don't see how the apoyando technique relates to a combination of melody and accompaniment, don Diego."

"It relates in two ways. Sometimes you accent a note in an arpeggio:

(bass notes optional)

"Other times you play a chord or a bass note together with an apoyando scale:

"Rest stroke is also used for playing two melodies at once."

"Let me see if I can play that . . . hmm, it's not easy to play a rest stroke and a thumbstroke at the same time."

"It takes a little work, all right, but it is well worth it."

"You can really hear the separation of the two lines."

"That's the value in it. But I think I have already given you a great deal to work with for one week . . . especially considering that you have some catching up to do . . ."

He paused significantly, to which I nodded.

"But why not?" he smiled. "Try this—focus your will on making

A TRANSFORMATION

a strong rest stroke, i–m–i–m, i–m–i–m. Then just try one thumb-stroke to the bar, like this.

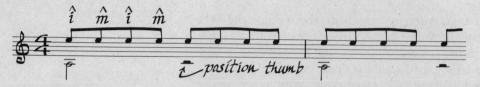

"My last word of advice, Alfonso, is this: Learn to play by touch, and not by sight. Check up on your left hand now and then, but do not be hypnotized by it. You tend not to concentrate on your sound if you concentrate on your sight.

"And now, I think we should call it a day."

"Oh yeah, it's 4:30 already—I've got to get going. Are you going to hike down with me?"

"I had planned on going later—playing again tonight, you know —but I don't mind going now, I guess."

"Aren't you concerned about the jaguar?" I said when I saw him pick up his guitar case, but not his weapons.

"The jaguar? Oh yes, of course."

He went to the kitchen and came back with a pistol stuffed in his belt.

"I think the jaguar's moved out, anyway, Alfonso. Let's go. Say, you didn't eat your biscuit."

"No, I'll take it along."

vii. A Slight Detour

During the walk down the mountain I ate the biscuit and don Diego recounted the part of his speech I missed by falling asleep Saturday evening, taking a more humorous tone than he had before. Other than that, there was nothing eventful about the hike, and I arrived at the bottom of the hill with a firm intention to return to my car immediately and head home. Don Diego was going in the same general direction I was, so both of us continued down the narrow street on the hill next to the church.

As soon as we entered the sheltered space between the high-walled buildings a pungent aroma wafted into our nostrils.

"Mm-mmh," don Diego sighed appreciatively.

"Delicious—what is that?"

"It's the Rincon, the restaurant at the end of the street. They start cooking dinner in the early afternoon—those roasts and pies can take hours, you know."

The scent of the good food was intoxicating. Except for the biscuits at don Diego's, and a piece of cake at the café on Saturday, I hadn't eaten in nearly 30 hours. All my senses seemed to have been sharpened by my hunger—one must picture the scene: The street was little wider than an alley, and a corridor of sky was marked out by the rooftops of the high buildings. The sun was low so the shadows between the buildings were dark, but the sky itself was brilliant, with pockets of turquoise between mountainous cumulus clouds. The air was cool and the rich aromas were warm and moist. I had never known such supreme sensual pleasure could be found in such simple sights and smells.

All my senses seemed to be heightened, except my sense of balance, unfortunately. In my olfactory rapture I failed to notice I was stepping into the gutter. When my foot hit the gutter bottom I tripped sideways, turned backwards and began to fall, pulling my guitar up to my chest. My tail received the worst of it in the end.

I looked at don Diego and he looked at me and we both started laughing.

"Are you all right there, Alfonso?"

"It only hurts when I laugh."

"Are you too weak to get up?"

"No, I'm going to get up as soon as I'm sure the street's stopped moving."

"Seems to me you're easily led by the nose, amigo," don Diego said while lending me a hand. With my backpack full of books and my tape recorder, I was a bit top heavy.

"No comment, don Diego, my dignity is bruised."

"I know how it is, the watchpig has bruised my dignity many times."

I was dusting myself off.

"You must be hungry, Alfonso. You shouldn't drive if you're hungry—what if you passed a bakery? There could be mayhem."

"I'll be OK as soon as I get on the road."

"No sir, you won't be OK, not unless you get something to eat. I insist you come along right now! I'm pretty hungry myself, so we're both going to eat."

"Oh, don Diego, I can't do that, not now."

"Nonsense, I'm treating you and you can't turn Venezuelan hospitality down, lest you insult the honor of my country."

"OK, what can I say? You win. I guess I am pretty hungry."

"Of course you are! I forget myself what it is like to have a youthful appetite, and I offer you biscuits as if they were a king's feast! Well, now we'll have some empanadas."

"And for dessert—fried bananas."

"Right."

LESSON VII:

The Land of the Lotus-Eaters

When we entered the Rincon I was surprised to see how well known and evidently popular don Diego was among the people there, customers and employees alike. It made sense, though, considering that he was an entertainer in their town and probably had been so for years. The odd thing was to see this facet of don Diego's personality brought into the light of day. To my complete surprise he was very congenial, smiling, making jokes and warm conversation, with never a hint of awkwardness or strain.

I bore this in mind when we sat down and ordered. I wanted to ask him some questions.

"Don Diego?"

"Yes?"

"You surprise me."

"How so?"

"I wouldn't have thought you were as much of a public figure as you are."

"Why not, because I don't take a bath often enough?"

"No, your philosophy, I guess."

"My philosophy?"

"What you said about loneliness and self-sufficiency. I just assumed that you would be . . . lonelier."

"Who says I'm not?"

"You don't seem to be, what with all these friends."

"Friends are worth more than gold, Alfonso—but there is nothing that can take away the fact of change. And it is the inexorable law of change that makes me stand alone and at the same time gives all the more value to my friends. To cling to a changing world is the height of foolishness, you see."

"I'll go along with that."

Don Diego chuckled. "Nice of you to agree, Alfonso." Then he peered into the table as if it were a deep, blue lake. "Lamentably, however, that lesson is built on top of many others you have yet to pass through."

"Like what?"

"Ah, here—the wine is coming."

"Like what, don Diego?"

"There are no words to tell you, Alfonso."

"That's ridiculous, everything meaningful can be put into words."

The waiter poured two glasses and left the bottle.

"*Gracias*, Ricardo."

"*Name* something that can't be put into words." I laughed and took a sip.

"Sure, Alfonso Fegoni couldn't be put into words, no matter how many you used."

"As long as you nailed down what kind of definition you wanted, you could do it."

"Look, Alfonso—suppose we got a whole roomful of professors, all right?"

"All right."

"Experts in everything, and we put them to work for ten solid years accumulating information, writing reports, and making experiments to define Alfonso Fegoni . . ."

"A waste of time, but OK."

"Do you think they could predict with any reasonable accuracy the next sentence to emerge from your mouth? Could they?"

I thought a second. "Maybe they could."

"I could have predicted you'd say that. So, are we going to let the wine just sit there? A toast, to your success in school."

"To your successful performance tonight."

"I'll drink to that."

We tipped our glasses.

"Name something else that can't be put into words, don Diego."

"Very well . . . music."

"Music? Hmm."

"Satisfied?"

"Now wait, I'm thinking."

"In a moment you'll tell me a piece of music can be analyzed down to a hieroglyphic code of numbers and formulas."

"It could—in fact, we can even build computers that turn out music."

"But that misses the point! The piece of music is a shadow cast by the flame of a man's spirit—it lives—the formulas are after the fact, they are *not* the fact."

"So what is spirit?"

"What is spirit, eh?"

"Yeah, this thing that casts the shadow? Can you point one out to me? Are you sure it's there? Maybe it's a bunch of brain cells, conspiring to play tricks on you."

"I'm sure it's there, but I can't show you one."

"There—that's where non-scientific thinking gets you."

"Where?"

"Into dreams, hallucinations, and superstitions."

"There is a saying, 'the spirit is that which dreams the dreams at night.' "

"What dreams the daydreams, then?"

"Alfonso Fegoni."

"Ho-ho-ho."

Don Diego sipped his wine. "What about . . . what about force, Alfonso?"

"Force?"

"Sure, you scientists talk about force all the time. Force of gravity, force of . . . I don't know—electricity."

"What about it?"

"Well, can you bring a force out and show me one? Can you point to a force? Can you touch, see, smell, taste, a force?"

"I can point to us sitting in our chairs, thanks to the force of gravity!"

"Well, I can point to music, thanks to the force of the spirit!"

"Touché. I'll toast to that, don Diego."

We refilled our glasses, and then the waiter brought out the dinner and set two heaping plates in front of us. An empanada turned out to be a kind of meat pie. If it had not been so hot, I would have been tempted to swallow it whole. I sat there, poking at it with my knife and fork.

"Listen, don Diego, I'll give you a good example of a night dream that's perfectly explainable without bringing spirit into it at all."

Don Diego had a forkful of empanada poised in front of his mouth.

"Do you want to hear?" I asked.

"Do you want to eat?" he replied.

"Yeah, but I want to tell you about this dream."

"What dream? Whose dream?"

"Mine."

"Well, why didn't you say so? I'm very interested."

"OK, this morning, before dawn, the birds woke me up, they were making so much noise."

Don Diego smiled and nodded.

"And I thought to myself, if only the mist came down—it might just put them back to sleep. And so, first thing I knew, I was falling asleep myself, dreaming about the mist. It filled up the room and made a tunnel for me to escape. Simple wish-fulfillment, right? So I walked into the tunnel. And at the end there was this pair of double doors. I walked right through—and do you know what I found?"

"What?"

"A bus terminal—filled with birds! I mean, the birds in the trees were just recast as people in a bus terminal."

"You mean they were people that looked like birds?"

"I mean they were *birds* acting like *people*. There were parakeets sitting on benches watching pay-TVs, there was a crow with glasses reading a newspaper, an old hen in a cloth coat who was looking at me like I was going to steal the bag cart she had alongside her . . ."

"Did they talk, then?"

"No, they were squawking and jabbering, just like birds. It was an incredible din."

"What do you make of that?"

"I think my mind just mixed the confusion of all this bird chatter outside your place with another confusing, noisy situation it knew about. Then it blended birds with people—because people belong in a bus station."

"What other 'people' did you see?"

"Oh, there was a rooster chasing after a couple of hens, and there was a coffee shop—The Capon Café, I remember—where there was a flamingo waitress, and a big, fat turkey frying eggs. It goes on and on."

"Did you stop in for a cup of birdseed?"

"No. This blue jay came up to me. He was wearing a denim jacket and he wanted a handout. He kept following me around asking for 'some bread.' "

"I thought they couldn't talk."

"They couldn't—it was squawking, but I understood. Anyway, I started yelling at him to leave me alone, but he wouldn't, and then some police started coming over . . ."

"Police?"

"Pelicans."

"Quite an aviary, Alfonso."

"Well, the dream was just using whatever birds fit the role. That's the point I'm making, this whole thing was a reflection of . . ."

"Go on, go on—I know the point you're making."

"Well, I broke into line with a bunch of parrots going through a door to a bus. But they all started flapping their wings and complaining. So the busdriver came over and started badmouthing me for causing a disturbance and disobeying the rules."

"What was he?"

I laughed. "A buzzard, a six-foot, bald-headed buzzard with black-framed glasses. He looked exactly like a professor of mine."

"Then do you think of your classmates as parrots?"

"No, no—but you know, you've kind of got to learn to be a parrot to succeed in the school game, sometimes."

"Hmm."

"Well, you came off a lot better than my professor, don Diego."

"Oh? I was honored to play a role in your dream?"

"Yes. I figure you came in about then and started to play guitar, because it was then that I ran out a door and climbed into an empty bus. You—I mean, this eagle—was driving, and a guitar was in the seat next to me. I started to play it while we drove off, and I was playing rather well, too—almost as well as you, I might add."

"A-ha!"

"Obvious case of wish-fulfillment. Now the bus was going up and up these ramps, which I think symbolizes the soothing effect your music was having."

"Mm-hmm."

"And, you know how you left the door open? Well, I think the cool breeze coming in gave my dream factory the idea for the mountains."

"What mountains?"

"The bus came out of a tunnel right onto a narrow road on the side of a huge mountain . . ."

"Was it day or night?"

"Night—night and there was a moon out, lighting the road."

Don Diego gave me a look which I took to be skeptical.

"No—it made sense—because by this time you were snoring."

He frowned.

"Well you were."

"Was I?"

"Snoring is a *night*time activity, isn't it?"

"I'll snore any damn time I please—go on."

"OK. Of course, I'd quit playing guitar by this time, and I noticed the driver seemed to be asleep at the wheel."

"Ah yes, the story of my life."

"Then I noticed something really funny—the Greyhound insignia was not really a greyhound—it was a . . . a bounding jaguar. And at the same time I noticed the sound of the engine—it was funny, too. I turned around, and there in the aisle, was a jaguar, purring loudly."

"I thought you didn't have any nightmares."

"Well, I was scared, just on principle, I guess. But there was something comical about it, too—the jaguar smiled—smiled and rolled over like a kitten. But like I said, I got scared so I began to wake up."

"A-ha. What do you make of this jaguar?"

"Well, here again, don Diego, this just illustrates how the mind is a computer. When the dream dissolved the purr remained, it followed me all the way into wakefulness, when it became, became your snoring. Now you've been telling me to watch out for the jaguar for weeks. Naturally the snore, because it was a foreign sound, was interpreted as something threatening, and my fear pulled in the jaguar as a symbol, forcing me to wake up and find out what was going on. Neat and simple."

"Neat, simple, and *wrong*," don Diego said, with a disquieting glance at me.

"What do you mean?"

"The jaguar . . . is a spirit guide."

"A spirit guide? Explain yourself."

"They sometimes visit us in dreams. You're lucky you had me to tell you what happened." Another forkful of empanada vanished in his mouth.

"Oh, for—a dream is a dream."

"Listen, it is harder to wake someone when they are dreaming than at any other time, no?"

"So?"

"It follows we are most detached from our senses when we are dreaming, does it not?"

"Maybe."

"Well, it is when we are detached from the senses that we are most receptive to communications from the beings inhabiting the subtler planes of existence. It is in dreams that spirit guides come to us and give us messages of profound importance! Except we usually forget or disbelieve when we wake up."

"But how do you know the jaguar was a spirit guide, presuming that there are such things?"

". . . Sometimes we are too stupid even to know what they are saying—How? How do I know? You seem to have overlooked the fact that every other creature in your dream, excluding yourself, was a bird."

"That sure isn't much."

"The purr of the jaguar—it was another telltale sign."

"How?"

"One of the irrefutable marks of a visitation dream is a vibration, or sound. Sometimes it is the ocean, or a white-water river, sometimes it is a wind that blows. . . . It could just as well be the purr of a jaguar, Alfonso."

I shrugged off a chill. The first dream—I remembered it well—the wind riffling the treetops. But then, it had been a windy day to begin with, so what was so surprising about finding a little breeze in my dream?

"Well, I'm unconvinced."

"There were other signs, too."

"Like what?"

"The moon."

"The moon? That's obvious—your last name, de Luna, the moon."

"Yes, but how do you think I *got* my name, eh? How do you think I *know* your jaguar is from the spirit plane?"

"You mean?"

"Yes, I've been to those mountains, too—I've seen the same moon myself!"

"And you saw, you saw a jaguar?"

Just then a voice came down from above.

"Can I get you gentlemen some dessert?"

"Oh, yes, Ricardo."

"What will it be, don Diego?"

"An order of fried bananas for my friend—is that all right, Alfonso?"

"Sure."

"And some custard for me, coffee, too."

"Make that two coffees," I said. "Aren't you going to have bananas?"

"No, tired of them, eat 'em practically every day."

"Oh, but what about the . . ."

"No. No, I did not see a jaguar."

"Describe your dream then."

"It wasn't a dream, Alfonso."

"What makes you so sure it was a visitation, then—the moon?"

"No, as I said—the sound."

"What sound?"

"In your case it was the purr of the cat, in mine it was the beating of a hummingbird's wings."

"That's pretty soft, isn't it?"

Don Diego shook his head, almost as if an ice cube had dropped down his back.

"No, not this one. It was so strong—it was paralyzing." He raised his hand and spread his fingers as if he were holding a crystal ball. "And it wasn't the hum you associate with beating air, Alfonso—it was electric—but rich, so rich in vibrations of the subtlest texture and hue, all of them audible with the utmost clarity. Is such a thing possible in a dream?"

"How vividly you remember."

"It happened a good fifty years ago, but I remember as if it were yesterday."

"Was there a message?"

"Nothing one could put into words, Alfonso."

"Try, why don't you."

"You might say he showed me my proper vocation. He took me to a place of barren rocks somewhere high on a mountain and showed me that there were really the seeds of beautiful plants and flowers among the sterile stones, like tiny, opalescent gems. His wings hummed a message to me—I was to raise them."

"Then that's how you realized that gardening was to be your life's work?"

"No."

"That gardening is a spiritual occupation?"

"No, I told you, I am a cultivator of spirits. Those were not literal flowers."

"Oh, I see."

"What struck me about your visitation was the moon—I shall never forget the bright, full moon that presided over the skies and the landscape."

"The moon in my dream wasn't full."

"Perhaps that means something."

Ricardo arrived with the bowl of custard, the fried bananas and the coffee. I started eating, looking for a way to shift the subject from spirit guides to something I was a little more comfortable with.

"I think you are denying what the spirit guide has to say to you, Alfonso."

"Can we perhaps discuss something else, don Diego?"

"Just let me say this, amigo . . ."

"What?"

"Steam down, son, listen to what I'm going to say—I won't say any more."

"OK."

"First of all, maybe you're right, it's all a dream."

I nodded my head.

"So if you're right it will do you no harm to wait a second, should that jaguar appear to you again—just refrain from panicking, hold your ground. If *I'm* right, you may learn something of great significance. If *you're* right—well, so what if he eats you?"

Don Diego downed a spoonful of custard.

I waited, expecting him to add something.

"Custard's excellent, Alfonso. How are the bananas?"

I took a bite. "Good, really good."

"What are you going to do then, Alfonso—if you see the jaguar again?"

"All right! I'll hang around until I see the whites of his eyes—satisfied?"

"Good."

"But I still say—a dream's a dream."

"A dream is a dream, quite right. . . ." Don Diego interrupted himself to wash the custard down with coffee. ". . . Whatever a dream is." He inhaled, sighed, raised his eyebrows and pulled out a cigar.

"Don Diego, Saturday you mentioned the Second Domain of Guitar Knowledge."

"Yes?"

"You said it was 'musical chemistry.' "

"Indeed so."

"Would you care to . . . to elaborate on that?"

He cast a glance in my direction.

"Though all sides of the guitarist are developed in the First Domain, the theme of its Three Realms is *technique*. In the Second Domain the guitarist continues to acquire technical and expressive power, but the theme is mental, analytical."

"Then there must be a Third Domain having to do with spirit."

"Yes. In the Second you learn the organization of musical sounds, and in the Third you will learn to apply your knowledge of musical chemistry and create your own compositions."

"Wow—terrific. What specifically is in the Second Domain?"

"Oh, many things—the Wheel of Fifths and the key system, transposition, modulation, the formulas of harmony . . .

"Whoa there! Eduardo!" don Diego interrupted himself.

A slightly built gentleman with a pencil-thin moustache and a leathery face had come in and was talking to the proprietor over the cash register. When he heard don Diego hail him he came over to the table.

"Eduardo, my friend, I would like you to meet Alfonso. Alfonso, this is Eduardo, the percussionist in our trio."

"Glad to meet you, Eduardo."

"My pleasure, Alfonso. You study guitar with don Diego, no?"

"Sí."

"You are privileged."

"Gracias."

Don Diego spoke up. "So, Eduardo, what is going on? Is José around?"

"I don't know—I thought maybe he was with you."

"Maybe he's back at La Fortuna."

"I hope so. I came out here to fetch the two of you. The place is jammed—we've got to go."

"That's unusual for a Sunday night—a big crowd."

"Couple of tourist buses."

"Well then, let's go. Alfonso, you are welcome to come, but otherwise, we must be off—you understand."

It was then that a clever idea took hold of me.

"I'll join you—but just for a little while."

"Bueno! Come then!"

We didn't even stop to pay. The proprietor, a fat, middle-aged man with bulging eyes who moved with the alacrity of a honey bear, just waved us past with the check held in his hand.

The restaurant where don Diego was to play was a good half-mile across town. We clambered into Eduardo's pickup truck and took off. It was a rattletrap if ever there was one, a testimony to the scarcity of replacement parts in that region. Every joint and bolt rattled, shook and creaked. The thing took curves like a battleship. The springs squeaked under the clutch and the brake had to be pumped two or three times to make it hold. Eduardo's face was cool as a card-sharking poker player's as he pumped the pedals, jammed the floor shift forward and back, and spun the wheel. As hair-raising as the ride was, it was a delight to watch him. Perhaps the wine was affecting me, but in the way he coordinated the pedals, wheel and levers, I could see how he played the drums, and could see that he was good, very good.

The drive must have been completed in less than a minute. I was barely able to catch up with the two of them as I finally fished my backpack from the shadows of the truckbed. Running in on their heels into the warmth, light, and liveliness of the restaurant, I was as exhilarated as I had ever been before in my life.

Feeling light-headed from the wine, stomach full, and still buzzing

147

from the ride, I nodded to don Diego as he and Eduardo went past the bar toward a door that led backstage. Then I began to search the front-row tables for a seat. None of those near the stage appeared to be unoccupied, but as I walked farther up the bar, craning my neck to see, I spied a single table with two unaccompanied young women sitting at it. "Tourists," I decided. They looked like Americans. "Perfect!"

I waded into the crowd with my guitar and backpack. When I came to the table I said hello, and they nodded and smiled. They also nodded when I motioned to the third chair, so I sat down across from them. I put my backpack on my lap and zipped it open. The girl across from me again smiled. Returning it was a pleasure—she was quite attractive, both of them were.

"Tape recorder," I said in English. "I'm tape recording my friends," I added when she looked inquisitive.

This girl looked at the other, then she said, *"Vi är från Sverige."*

"Oh! You're Swedish, then?"

"Ja—kommer du från USA?"

"Yes, I mean, *ja.*"

"Talar du Svenska?" she asked, and both of them were amused by my bewildered expression. "Speak Svedish?" she said with a lilting accent. I smiled and shook my head. She laughed and said something to her friend. Her friend nodded.

Their names were Britt and Gunnel, but an exchange of names was about as far as the conversation could move for the moment, especially in the noisy environment. They began to converse between themselves while I searched my backpack for my microphone. I noticed them giggling, and I thought it might well involve me, for it had been two and a half days since I'd changed clothes, showered or shaved.

Nevertheless, I had my plan, and that was plenty to occupy my attention. Reaching inside the knapsack, I pulled the tape recorder around to where I could see the mode switches and recording level dials. Then I inserted the microphone jack into its plug, and dragged the microphone out by its wire. "Well, Melinda, here you go," I thought gleefully.

Before making the next move I smiled at my tablemates, then I ducked under the table to put the tape recorder out of sight. Very soon I heard the sound of feminine knuckles rapping on the table above. "Cute," I thought. The next thing I heard was a familiar voice booming down from above.

"Alfonso, what the hell are you doing under there?"

I quickly put the microphone on the floor and sat up with as much dignity as I could muster. Don Diego stood over me with his fists on his hips.

"Tying my shoes," I said.

"Do you girls speak Spanish?" he asked, turning to them sweetly. Britt shrugged her shoulders. *"Vi är från Sverige,"* offered Gunnel.

Don Diego smiled and nodded. *"Gracias,"* he said to them. Then he turned to me. "Tying your shoe, eh? What do you take me for, a two-legged llama? I know what you were up to."

"Really, don Diego, I can explain." I thought for sure he'd seen the tape recorder.

"If you want to look at their thighs, Alfonso, you can surely think up a more discreet way than that, *caramba,* for all your brains."

"Oh, well, don Diego, you know how it is." My relief was substantial.

Don Diego leaned over, putting one hand on the back of my chair, the other on the table.

"Say, Alfonso, you don't speak their language, do you?"

"Uh, no."

"How do you expect to get to know them, then?"

I held up my right hand and shook my head.

"Well, I doubt very much you're encouraging the process by 'tying your shoe.' And, my friend Alfonso—do you have any idea how you look?"

I scratched my chin—the bristles were well advanced.

"You need a comb?" he inquired.

"I've got a comb."

"Take a good peek at that one on the left," said don Diego, looking at the stage. He was referring to Britt. "Don't go looking at her directly, you fool. Pretend you're listening to me and then look around the room . . . see? Beautiful, eh? She's a lady with class. I'll bet she's a college student just like yourself."

"She does look intelligent."

"If only you could talk to her—the things you could say . . . I'll bet you could tell her a lot about the force of attraction, eh?"

"Oh come on, lay off."

"I can tell you just what she's thinking now, Alfonso."

"You can?"

"Yes. She's thinking you are a typical, youthful American clown who believes he's finding himself by coming to a foreign country, running out of money, and neglecting to wash and shave himself. With your backpack and guitar, you're a classic case—she feels sorry for you."

"Thanks a lot."

"But . . . besides that—she thinks you're cute."

"She does? How do you know?"

"I *know*, that's how. And I'll tell you something else about her— she'd like to get to know you."

"She would?"

"I think she finds you interesting."

"Yeah?"

"Listen, do you think she's come all the way to South America from her country . . ."

"She's Swedish."

"Careful, Alfonso. If she knows three words in a foreign tongue, it's probably no, no, and the name of her country. I don't want those chicas to think we're talking about them. Keep your eyes on the stage, please. That's my man. Now, do you think she's sacrificed a bankroll, left her native land, and come on this long journey without expecting somewhere along the trail something exciting will happen in the way of romance?"

"I guess . . . I guess it's not unlikely."

"And don't you think it likely that after she has traveled about South America, finally to arrive unescorted at this remote and romantic little town, her insides are wound taut as violin strings waiting to have pretty melodies bowed from them?"

I couldn't answer a word. I stared at the stage and I could feel the blood rushing to my forehead as I projected don Diego's salty speculations onto the radiant young girl across from me. Britt was a light brunette, tall and fair-skinned with piquant freckles. Her eyes were green and lively, her Scandinavian face round with high cheekbones and refined features. Her upper lip had been sculptured in a graceful peak, giving her a sensual look. She exuded health and freshness—one could picture her riding a horse or thoughtfully reading a book, and looking equally provocative in either case.

I gave a quick glance in her direction. Her attention was elsewhere, but by chance the nostrils of her retroussé nose flared slightly just then. I put my right hand to my temple and looked at the floor.

"Don't doubt it, Alfonso. She must have spent a small fortune on this lark, and she is probably aware as she can be that now is the prime of her life and she won't be this way again for a long time to come. She's yearning to have the time of her life—but not by way of shallow thrills—she has taste and sensitivity. And you might be able to give her an experience to remember with the highest pleasure—you might even start something grand with her, who knows? You have the spirit to do it—and you can get across to her what you have and what you are, in spite of your seedy appearance and the fact that you cannot speak her language."

"H-how?"

"You can use the universal language—the language of music."

"Surely you don't mean I should get out my guitar here and now and play?"

"*Now*, yes, but not *here*—up *there!*" and he pointed to the stage.

"*You* must be *kidding.*"

"I'm not kidding. Lord, I wish I was in your shoes, and that I had a chance to . . . but I've had my day in the sun, and now I'm making an opportunity for you, and that makes me feel very good, too."

"Don Diego, you can't seriously expect me to play solo guitar up there—you know that I . . ."

"Not solo. In the group. José isn't coming tonight. I came out here to tell you that you might as well go home and come another time, when we are working together as a unit."

"Why didn't José come?"

"Sudden emergency—his wife's having a baby. But when I found you here alone with these beautiful girls, that one on the left in particular, it dawned on me that there's a method to our misfortune. This was no accident, this was . . ."

"Now wait a minute—it's quite a leap from José's wife's blessed event to me getting up on that stage to lay one, *big, fat* egg!"

"What makes you think you will lay an egg?" He sounded almost as if he believed himself.

"You must be joking—I can't play worth a bean and you know it!"

"Don't talk that way about one of my guitar apprentices."

"Very funny—but it's still true."

"*Bulería!* You only *think* you can't play worth a bean."

"I can't."

"When you play out of your brain you surely can't, but when your hands are driven by spirit, you are altogether another kind of artist."

"Sure, like the first time we met when you got me to thromp the guitar half to death?"

"That was one time. It was before you knew of the Three Realms of Guitar Knowledge. Don't forget the strums you improvised at the next lesson or . . ."

"More chaos."

". . . or this morning, when you played like a journeyman expert in the Three Realms."

"This morning? You were listening to me?"

"I was highly impressed."

"You never said a word though."

"That was strictly a conversation between you and the mountains, the gathering clouds, and the trees. I had no business commenting on it."

"But now?"

"Now I see you letting an opportunity slip past you."

"The opportunity to make a fool of myself?"

"To convert the conversation you had with the mountains to a conversation with other human souls."

"You're talking . . ."

"Not to mention your friend over there."

". . . you're talking out of my league."

"No, you see what has happened this weekend is a sequence of events too meaningful to be just coincidence. Now it is up to you to finish the fabric."

"Why don't I just say it? I'm too AFRAID to go up there . . . what am I going to do?!" My feet were getting very itchy.

"I'm telling you, you don't have to worry about it. I can explain to you . . ."

"I won't do it, and that's final! I'm taking my guitar and going home. I have to get out of here."

"Alfonso!"

"Yes?"

"You go home now and you deny the gift of gold the forces of spirit have brought to you. You deny them and you deny me as your teacher—if you go out that door you are telling me you have no trust and no faith in me and my forty years of experience. You walk now, and you walk out of the apprenticeship you have been granted."

I looked up at don Diego. He was serious, there was not the slightest doubt about it.

"Why don't you take your fear by the tail and laugh in its face, Alfonso, my friend?"

"Ha-ha," I said drily.

"Aren't these people out here really just a bunch of computers, anyway? That's what you insisted on at dinner, eh. Don't tell me you're going to allow yourself to be intimidated by a drunken band of computers, are you?!

"Just like you to joke when you're serious."

"Which is it, Alfonso? Going home? Or staying?"

We faced off in silence, then I looked down.

"How long?"

"As long as you want."

"OK, OK, I'll do it. For Chrissakes, why make such a big deal out of it?"

Don Diego patted my cheek.

"Bueno, now come, follow me—we've got to tune up."

Don Diego smiled and nodded to the girls, then turned and started back. I stood up, and as I did so my right heel came to rest on the microphone. I felt the crunch through my foot, and stood still a second with my eyes closed.

Don Diego turned around. "Change your mind?"

"No," I replied and grabbed my guitar from under the table, kicking the fractured microphone to the side. I made motions to Britt and Gunnel to see if they would watch my backpack for a minute, and they agreed.

"But don Diego," I said, catching up to him at the door near the bar, "are you going to play anything in any keys other than C and G?"

"Of course, that's right—you don't know any keys except C and G."

"Well, then I guess you can't use me after all."

He took me by the elbow and we went on through into a hall near the kitchen.

"Sit down here, Alfonso."

He meant on the head of a nearby pickle barrel. Then he took out his guitar, put his foot on a chair, and set the guitar across his thigh. He tuned it up lightly and quickly, strummed an E chord once or twice and then spoke.

"All right, you're going to learn to play in all the keys right now."

"Are you serious? You're not serious."

"There is a quick and easy way to do it—a way special to the guitar. You won't know what notes you are playing, but nevertheless it works for every key immediately."

"I can't believe that's possible, not after . . ."

"First of all: chords. Here, get your guitar out, tune to mine. Better yet, you take mine, and I'll tune yours."

When don Diego handed my tuned guitar back to me, I felt like a raw recruit who has had a rifle slapped into his hands by the D.I. with orders to break it down in ten seconds flat.

"Now here is a G major 7 chord; this is F ♯ major 7; and this is A♭ major 7.

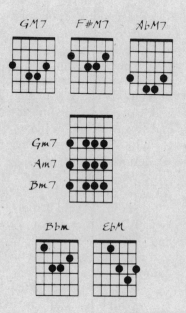

"You see? All you have to do is slide the chord up or down the neck. It doesn't matter what the chord quality is. Here are G minor 7, A minor 7, and B minor 7.

"All of these chords are named for the note on the sixth string."

"I saw that."

"Good. Some are fifth string, or fourth string chords. For example, A minor raised one fret becomes B♭ minor, or B minor at the second fret, or C minor at the third—whatever the note is on the fifth string. D Major raised one fret becomes E♭ major, and so on . . ."

"Can you do this with all the chords?"

"If they don't have open strings, yes. You must damp any open strings by leaning the fingers of your left hand. But do not get concerned, I am going to show you the chords before each song."

"You mean I'm supposed to learn them on the spot?"

"You can do it—there are not as many different chords as you probably think—didn't I hear you say once that you knew dozens, maybe hundreds of chords?"

"I guess I did. But don Diego, I don't know—what about scales? How am I going to learn them in the next two minutes?"

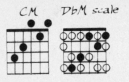

"Scales are movable too. For example, if you slide the C scale points up one fret, you are in the key of D flat. Whatever you can play in C, you can play in D♭, just by using the same fingering pattern, or scale form, if you please."

"But don Diego—this is hopeless! Even if I understood what you're saying, and in principle I think I do—I still couldn't pluck the notes out of my brain and pin them to the right places in the scale form! That takes training—you saw the way I goofed up 'Twinkle, Twinkle, Little Star!' "

"You won't have to do any scale playing you don't want to, Alfonso. Eduardo is taking care of the rhythm, I'm taking care of the melody—you're in between, taking care of the harmony. You can pick up your cues from Eduardo—you don't have to carry the whole weight of the beat, you can just strum here and there to ornament Eduardo's work. You'll sound incredibly good doing very little. You see? You have the two of us flanking you—you can't fail."

Just then Eduardo came out of the kitchen, eating a chicken leg.

"Are you ready to go yet, Diego?"

"Not quite."

"Are you going to help us out, Alfonso?" he added.

"Sí, I'm going to try."

"You're going to try? That's good, I'm glad you're going to try," he nodded. "You try your best, OK? And if you screw up?" He took the bone away from his mouth and looked for a shred of meat to tear at. "We going to boil you like a chicken." He smiled at me.

"Here, you want a glass of wine?" he said, and handed me his glass. Then he went down the hall.

"He's gone to get his stuff . . . hey, Alfonso, don't let him bother you! Eduardo just talks like that—you know, it's his style—it means he likes you."

"I'd hate to see what he's like when he doesn't like you!"

Don Diego laughed.

"I don't see how I can go through with this."

"You're afraid."

"I'm afraid," I answered and drank a slug of wine.

"Good! You should be afraid."

"Good, huh?"

"What's more, you should accept your fear, and breathe it like oxygen. It is going to give life to your performance. I'm going to start worrying the day I am not afraid to perform any more."

"You're afraid?"

"Yes, sure."

"You sure don't look it."

"No, I'm not *worried*—that's the difference. I *like* getting into situations. What does fear do for you in the woods, eh? It makes you alert, sensitive, fast, sure. Fear is your friend. I can't understand people wanting to get rid of their butterflies. Look, if you're bound to do something, committed, what good is it to be mentally running from it, while physically staying—you're paralyzed, the thing you fear comes true . . ."

I took a great gulp of wine.

"Maybe you shouldn't drink any more," said don Diego. "It will make you fumble."

THE LAND OF THE LOTUS-EATERS

"Fumble? Look at me now . . ." I held out my hand. "How am I going to play when my hands are like that?"

"Say, you're shaking like a leaf, Alfonso," don Diego laughed.

I folded my arms across my chest and looked down.

"Alfonso, I'm telling you, all you need is belief in yourself. Look, if you fail, it is nothing to me personally, but it does reflect on our group and the management here, and I have to think of that. And I *have* thought of that—so, would I risk putting you on stage with me and Eduardo if I really expected you to blow our reputation? If *I* believe in you, why won't *you*? But I can see the truth isn't going to penetrate your mind in time, so I want to do something extra to ensure your chances of success. Let me . . ."

"Don Diego, we're just going in circles, nothing's going to do any goo . . ."

I stopped, responding to something being held out in front of my downturned face. Don Diego finished his sentence.

"Let me offer you this, a Cigar of Power."

The object was a slender stogie, black and tarry looking, which don Diego was extending, poised upright between his gathered fingers.

Eduardo was coming back with a heavy suitcase in one hand, a large drum under his other arm. As he passed he looked at don Diego and they nodded to each other. He went up the steps to the stage door.

"Cigar of Power? Is this a joke, don Diego?"

"It is no joke. If you feel you cannot maintain yourself out there, and you don't want to resign in defeat, you have this alternative—you may smoke the Cigar of Power. It is treated with a combination of rare herbs and plant extracts from the jungles of the south and the mountains of the north of our country. The mixture must be cured for two years before the poison turns to potency. Don't inhale it in the lungs. Just treat it like a cigar. It will rapidly penetrate into the bloodstream through the mouth."

"With what effect?"

"It will temporarily, for a couple of hours, give you the ears of a bat, and raise the power of your musical brain by fiftyfold."

"If I smoke it, will I be able to drive?"

"Oh, you'll drive better than ever . . ."

"Come on, Diego."

It was Eduardo, leaning through the stage door.

"Are you ready, Alfonso?"

"Ready as I'll ever be, I guess."

And so, tagging on de Luna's heels, I climbed the two short steps to the door, and walked out on the stage.

It was a modest little arena (to be slaughtered in). We were actually somewhat cramped with only the three of us on board. I slipped the crooked black cigar into my shirt pocket and beheld, with gut-wrenching dread, the audience that a moment ago I had used to protect me in my little scheme to record don Diego. I felt completely stripped of my usual sense of control. My eyes flashed back to the table where Britt and Gunnel sat. They were looking directly at me. Britt's eyes were twinkling and she was smiling. This made me feel encouraged in spite of everything and I smiled back.

Eduardo still hadn't put his gear in order. He had several different kinds of ethnic drums, plus an odd assortment of shakers, raspers, chimes, and cymbals. While he adjusted the arrangement of these things I sat down on my heels next to my guitar case and snapped it open. From second to second I had no idea of what was coming next. Don Diego knelt down beside me with his guitar in hand.

"OK, Alfonso, this is the chord progression to our first song. The first eight bars use G major 7, F# half-diminished 7, B7♭9, and E minor 7. That's repeated twice, then we go to the B section. The chords for the B section are . . ."

I sighed.

"Hey, listen—this is it! Get your hand working while I'm talking."

Don Diego took another five minutes getting me to repeat after him. I was to enter with a syncopated strum when Eduardo had gone four bars solo. Then, after four more bars of both of us, don Diego was to join with his guitar and voice. Both Eduardo and don Diego were going to sing. I thanked god de Luna wasn't asking me to sing as well.

Don Diego stood up and made the introduction. He bantered over the heads of the audience with a few regulars by the bar, and told a joke that produced general laughter. Since I knew she did not understand, I smiled at Britt and when she smiled back, some of my fear actually began to convert to excitement—what if I *could* pull it off? The wine I had imbibed a moment ago was circulating in my veins, warming me, making me feel a little bolder. With no way back, I was suddenly glad to be there. I was going to give it my best shot.

Don Diego looked at Eduardo and gave him the beat. Eduardo began patting and thumping the drums. One bar, two, three bars, four-two-three-four—and my hand went down on One, up on And.

And then I was lost! I wasn't sure where I was in the measure or when the next one was going to start. I missed the chord change, fumbled to catch up and then sped ahead, coming to the E minor 7 too soon.

The beat broke down, Eduardo stopped. Don Diego looked at me, then at Eduardo, and tapped the beat again.

Eduardo played his introduction, I looked at the restless audience with the horrible sensation that panic was about to break through my thinning defenses. With great deliberateness I came in on time and survived my four bars until don Diego arrived.

We made it through the song, but only by playing with the squarest of half-note rhythms was I able to hold down my end of it. It was clear we were losing the audience, and it was my fault. Don Diego went into action to save the act. Rather than take any time to huddle with me, he announced that he was going to do a guitar solo.

With lightning speed and a sensitive command of the dynamics, he strummed out a lyrical progression of chords. That brought silence upon the house immediately. Then he began expanding on the theme with scale and arpeggio runs to which there were always unexpected and interesting melodic twists.

I sat on the stool wondering what I could do. I knew if I stayed I was doomed to bungle again and perhaps make a farce out of everything. I was afraid of humiliating Eduardo and don Diego, but if I left now I'd have to leave in disgrace. I didn't want to look at the audience, much less at Britt, whose smile had encouraged me just minutes before. I had confirmed what don Diego had surmised was in the mind of that beautiful and self-possessed young woman, that I was a clown who didn't know what he was doing.

Then I noticed the Cigar of Power resting in my shirt pocket. I'd forgotten about it. I took it out and sniffed it again. Besides the tobacco scent, it had a certain sweetness, like that of flower blossoms. Just then an orange glow appeared on my hand, and I felt some warmth near my cheek. Eduardo, with his card-shark's immobile face and pincer moustache, was holding out a lighted match. Did he know that this was a Cigar of Power? Did it really matter?

The decision was made impulsively, but at that moment, under those circumstances, I saw no other way. I put the cigar in my mouth and sucked in a few puffs.

Eduardo shook out the match and sat back down as if nothing significant had taken place.

I took in a mouthful of smoke. It did smell different, milder and more aromatic than don Diego's cigars. I took another puff and another. I noticed that the audience had completely forgotten me. They were under the spell of don Diego's guitar.

I looked out on the mass of faces, letting my eyes wander to the darkened rear of the room. People moved there in the shadows—a waitress or two, a customer picking his way through the tables. I looked away again, but just as I looked away my eyes brought a bizarre image to my brain—all those shadows in the back—they looked like the silhouettes of enormous birds. When I glanced back, all was normal again.

I held the cigar out in front of me and frowned at it. I was feeling light-headed now, beyond a doubt. The birds again? What now—hallucinations?

There was nothing to laugh at, I was still in the same perilous spot I had been before, and yet I felt like laughing. The audience was for some reason a comical sight—they were all so wrapped up in don Diego's guitar solo. Their stilled faces were amusing.

"A guitar solo is great, but why . . ."

And then, almost midsentence in my thoughts, they came flying at me, through me, like a spray of sparkling lights—the notes, the *real* notes, no longer pretty tones strung together in the air, but cargo-carrying vessels, chains of meanings within meanings telling legends of the lands and realms within don Diego's heart.

I looked at the old guitar player and I was awed. Did he know what he was doing? I looked at de Luna's eyes, and by the minute changes in his expression, I could tell that he did indeed know what he was doing, he knew full well. He was in control of every nuance of tone duration and volume and he was manipulating them with an intuitive precision impossible to describe. What I was seeing and hearing then I felt could not be true—the man's spirit had expanded like a glowing star to fill the room and it was held there, circulating and burning with intensity, by a wooden box, some tightly drawn cords, and the gymnastics of his hands and fingers.

Then I looked out at the audience—did they see what I saw, hear what I heard? I decided they couldn't be, for surely their mouths would have been hanging open, too, and their eyes would have been as wide as mine.

Now, some ten minutes after they had begun their journey, the inspired fingers fanned into a crescendo of scales and then strums, and finally brought the vibrating strings to a ringing conclusion. The sound died away, and the applause immediately rose up in its place.

In the midst of the uproar, I walked up to don Diego and I shook his hand.

"There's only one word for what you are, don Diego—you are a Wizard, a Wizard."

"A Wizard—I like that title. Thank you, Alfonso. And now, while they're still happy, you better let me show you the chords to the next song."

"Lead on."

From there forward, everything changed. I picked up the chord progression accurately in no time, and played it as if I'd rehearsed for weeks. With each succeeding song I grew bolder in my use of rhythms. Then I began fingerpicking the chords, too—it was as if I was rising right up through the Three Realms all over again. But the Cigar of Power had done more than that. It now seemed I was drawing on a fund of knowledge I never knew I had access to. I could have gone back later and figured out why I did the things I did, but at the time I did them it was under the influence of a higher, instantaneous, logic.

The attitude of the audience changed completely as the band began to function as a unit. The faces that had been turned toward one another in conversation were more and more turned toward the stage. At times hands were clapping, whistles and whoops erupted—some people even got up and danced in the aisle by the bar. But when silence was needed, as in some of the slow songs and instrumentals, there was silence, which was probably the greatest compliment of all.

I felt like a battery drawing power from Eduardo and don Diego and all the people beyond the foot of the stage. My courage reached its peak during one of don Diego's extended solos. I was strumming the chordal accompaniment, as had been my role all evening, when I received a look from Britt. It may have been the thirtieth occasion that night of such a mutual locking of eyes, but this time I felt I had to show her how she made me feel, so when don Diego's melodic drive slowed into the eighth bar cadence, I bid to take over the lead with an imitative run of notes played dedillo.

Don Diego looked over at me while Eduardo's drums carried the beat, then he answered back with a clipped variation. I made a one-bar comment in another range, then he turned the comment upside down. On we went, trading thoughts, and I began playing with more force, until don Diego simply took to strumming chords while I made my guitar sing. It seemed my fingers could do no wrong—they were drawn magnetically to the right marks; and when the chorus came around the last time, all three of us, yes, even I, sang in harmony. By the time we came to the closing chord I was in a delirium of musical blissfulness, strumming faster and faster and still faster, until my hand disappeared into a blur . . .

Suddenly, the A string snapped—pop!

Some people near the front saw, and laughed, among them my new girl friends, but the sound was like a rifle shot to me. I looked at my watch for the first time since dinner and a wave of panic went through me—12:00 midnight! I had to get the hell out of there! How had I let the time go by like this?

I got off my stool, thrust my guitar into the nearby case, and latched the top down, with the A string caught dangling outside. The applause had just begun when I stood up and faced don Diego, who was standing immediately behind my back with his guitar under his right arm. He grabbed my right shoulder and said, "Bravo! Well done! When I told you this was your opportunity, did I tell you wrong? What now? Are you going?"

"Well, don't you think it's time? Or do you think there's some part of my destiny I haven't fulfilled yet?"

"Why are you angry?"

"I'm not angry—I'm just disgusted with myself for being so stupid as to let myself . . . oh, never mind."

I pulled away and jumped off the stage. Going to my table, I quickly grabbed my backpack from underneath, stuffing the broken microphone back inside. When I stood up Britt was regarding me with a cool curiosity while Gunnel talked to someone at a neighboring table.

"Music was nice—thank you!" Britt said. I read in her eyes she was unhappy she could not say more. I hesitated as I thought of writing out my name and address, but contemplating another moment's delay only incensed me over the consequences of my frivolity once again.

"Well, nice meeting you," I said. "Good-bye."

Gunnel turned back and smiled. "Good-bye!" they both said.

Hesitating for another second I then turned and started making my way toward the door. Don Diego caught up with me just before I reached the end of the bar.

"What's wrong, amigo? This was a night of victory for you, you are a triumphant success—you should be happy!"

"I am happy, don Diego—I am—but look, I can't stand here and talk to you about it, and if I do, I'm liable to get very mad . . . at myself. I'm late, don't you see? So let me go, I'll be OK, I just have to get out of here."

"You're mad already."

"I am not! Now let me go, will you for once just let me do what I want to do?"

"OK, Alfonso, OK. We'll talk next week, eh? You're tired now."

"Yeah." I turned and started walking out.

"Do you know where your car is from here?"

"I'll find it!"

"Hey, drive carefully, eh?"

And with that I passed into the lobby and out of sight of don Diego. Two jovial and slowly sauntering Venezuelans had just entered the restaurant as I came to the door. I stood aside impatiently, and then ran out.

As I emerged, an unexpectedly gusty wind picked up the nose of my guitar case and tossed it to the side, then grabbed the tail and pushed it back the other way. I looked up at the sky. The stars were blotted out by a mass of roiling black clouds. I put down my knapsack, pulled out my sweater and proceeded up the street. My car was back most of the way toward the Rincon, and I ran the entire distance. By the time I inserted the key in the lock, a fine sprinkle had begun to fall. As I opened the trunk and put my guitar inside, the sky flickered, illuminating the street in a pale, electrical hue.

I shut the trunk and walked around to the front of the car. Just as I slid into the front seat, the thunderclap arrived. I slammed the car door, put the key in the ignition, pumped the pedal and turned the engine over. It caught, and I released the emergency brake. We began to roll. The time was 12:17.

By 12:30 I was negotiating the treacherous winding curves of Camino Cielo while bucking a fierce headwind. Every few moments a bolt of lightning flashed overhead, making the rim of the canyon stand out like a pair of black jaws against the sky. The booming thunder rolled down without delay, inundating the car, rattling it like a tin box.

I knew it was going to be a long drive home—but I had no idea then that it was to be the most harrowing night of my life. The night before was to become a picnic by comparison. At that point I was preoccupied with only two things: keeping the car on the road and staying awake. Neither was very easy. The blustering wind pushed the vehicle this way and that, shaved off 25 percent of my speed, then gave it back in a rush. I leaned forward over the wheel and raised my brow. The rain was blinding, but more than that, it seemed—after a nearly sleepless span of 60 hours—that consciousness might very well flee within the blink of an eye.

It was because of these conditions I missed the turnoff at the base of the canyon, continuing in the wrong direction for nearly an hour before discovering my error. Fortunately—or so I thought—I found an easy way back to the main highway. It led over the hills and through Infierno, a small town in the industrial district. But it was in Infierno that my misfortunes began in earnest. I reached the place around 2:30 in the morning. I admit to being overwhelmed with joy when I saw the freeway entrance down the street ahead. The street was empty—who could blame me for leaning on the accelerator a little bit?

The police of Infierno, unfortunately, did not see things this way.

There is no reason to complain loud and long about what happened. I only desire to make it clear how it was I came to stay up all night that night. Due to my fatigue, my Spanish was less than fluent. In fact my responses to the officer's questions resembled those of a drunk's. Nor did my appearance impress them as too reputable I'm sure.

Suffice it to say I spent the rest of the night in a cage, wringing my hands. But about 7 A.M. I was finally able to persuade them to just let me pay the fine for speeding and drive off, promising to carry with me a new and lasting respect for the traffic laws of Venezuela.

I reached school at 9:10 A.M. As I hurried across campus with my papers under my arm, I hoped and prayed that Forzosa would not have left by the time I got to the lecture hall. But then I began to wonder if the real tragedy would be if he had stayed. After 72 sleepless hours it was doubtful I could even deliver a straight sentence, let alone present a coherent discussion. As I was about to push open the doors to the room I almost changed my mind. I was thinking of my appearance—three days without a change of clothes or a bath—I looked and smelled like a bum! My comb was even missing. But then I considered what it would do to my reputation if I failed to show at all. And so I pushed the door open and walked through.

Not six feet in front of me, marching up the aisle, was Professor Forzosa.

"Good day, Mr. Fegoni," he said as he approached.

"Are you leaving, Dr. Forzosa?"

"Do you expect me to wait fifteen . . . minutes . . . ?" he said, beginning to eye me up and down.

I began to panic. My threshold was pretty low at that moment.

"Dr. Forzosa, I'm sorry, I'm really sorry but, but I can explain

THE LAND OF THE LOTUS-EATERS

everything." I wanted to defend myself logically, but self-pity got the better of me. "I . . . I've been running without sleep for three days straight, you see—and last night—a terrible thing—I was caught by a storm in the mountains. I nearly went off the road—totally exhausted —but that's not the worst of it—I had to spend the rest of the night in a jail cell. It's a miracle I made it here at all . . ."

Forzosa's frown could have fried eggs. I immediately compounded my error.

"But I am prepared, fully prepared, to give my talk in spite of all this. It's not like it sounds, anyway, really—they thought I was drunk —heh, heh—but I wasn't. It was all fatigue. A glass of wine or two was all I'd had before I left the bar. Anyone can drink that much—and it was all hours before, you see."

"Enough, enough of this nonsense. Let me by."

I stood aside and Forzosa marched out the door. The faces of the six or seven people who had shown up for the talk were turned my way, except one party who was sleeping. My head was pounding and there was a feeling like having a tight bandage wound around my chest.

"Damn it!" I cursed under my breath, and started out into the hall. When I came to Forzosa's office he was already there, just seating himself in his armchair under the cases of colorful moths and butter-flies.

"Mr. Fegoni, it would behoove you to knock before entering my office!" he said angrily.

"I'm . . . I'm sorry, Dr., sir. I couldn't leave things hanging like that. I want to apologize for my behavior—but you must understand."

"Understand what, Mr. Fegoni? That the poor performance you started out with is just deteriorating steadily? That you are talking and acting like an idiot? I can see that for myself!"

"No, sir."

"Well, what then? What do you have to say for yourself?"

"I . . . I don't know, Dr. Forzosa. I don't know anymore."

"Then I should like you to leave for the time being. I shall have to deal with this matter later, after I give it some thought. We cannot tolerate this kind of behavior."

"Now wait, please. I prepared for today's lecture—I really did. I studied all week, and for that matter, all weekend. What's happening isn't fair. I am truly a victim of circumstance."

"Look, Mr. Fegoni—I can see you are under a lot of stress. I've been noticing how distracted you've been all quarter. It is even conceivable you are going through some sort of breakdown. *But*, your personal problems do not concern me. It may sound cold, but it is a fact that it is not my role nor that of the school to hold your hand or play mother or father to you. We are set up to train scientists in this institution, and *that* is our purpose. It is in a manner of speaking, a business, and it strikes me that you are not a very committed member of the group."

"Dr. Forzosa, ever since the quarter began, you've been getting the wrong impression of me. But I think you've been too hasty in making up your mind."

"You'd better explain yourself."

"Well . . . well, for example—just because I've carried a guitar around with me from time to time, that doesn't mean I'm not serious about the program here. I am, I love science!"

"What are you talking about?!"

Now, thinking he wanted me to explain how a guitar player and a scientist are not necessarily incompatible identities, I launched into a speech, a speech that doomed me.

"There's no reason to—you needn't think that a guitar player and a scientist aren't . . . I mean, they are not all that different at the root—in spirit. That is, there's a certain similarity between the sense of excitement one has over the beauty of creation—not only the creative act, but of all Creation—and the excitement that one can derive from music—though it's subjective, I know it's subjective, and science is objective—but it's the same as, or not unlike, the thrill of a scientific discovery. When you talk about why people go into science—maybe it's that same desire to transcend the limitations of ordinary life! That spirit could be the most important thing about science—pure science. It has always motivated me—all the great geniuses talk about it—but with so much emphasis on grades . . . but now that's getting onto another subject altogether. What I'm saying is, you've formed the wrong impression. I am serious, I am committed. . . ."

"Mr. Fegoni!" said Dr. Forzosa, who was on his feet, leaning forward, his hands braced on the desk. "What you are rambling on about has about as much to do with *science* as *comic* books have to do with *great literature!* Now *you* may think you have demonstrated your genius . . ."

"I didn't mean that!"

"But *I* think you are a *lunatic!* And this is not an asylum! Now I want you to clear out of my office. I want you to leave, and I don't want to see you here until 10 A.M. Wednesday, at which time my secretary will have the necessary papers made up to take care of your dismissal from the Department of Chemical Engineering."

"You're going to kick me out?"

"Mr. Fegoni, approving your admission was one of two or three such mistakes I've made in the *history* of my tenure—and certainly the grossest. Now go. Good luck to you, and shut the door on your way out—please!"

My eyes were swollen when I opened them. I saw the luminous dial of the clock in the darkness—a quarter to midnight. I'd been asleep for 14 hours.

Fourteen hours! As I began to wake up, the recollections of what had happened in the lecture hall and Forzosa's office came back to me like a bad dream.

"But it isn't a dream! What have I done?!" I whispered aloud. "No, what has don Diego done with his Cigar of Power!"

I got up and started pacing the floor.

"I was drugged—that's the only way I could have acted so absurdly."

I paced some more.

"What now? What now? I have to go back and apologize—no, it will never work—I'm finished. Finished! I'll have to go back to the States. What am I going to tell my mom and dad? What about all the money that was spent?

"Why, if I hadn't met de Luna, none of this would ever have happened. I wouldn't have been late for my first appointment with Forzosa. I wouldn't have been carrying the guitar around with me, or practicing when I should have been studying. The manipulation was subtle, but he showed his true colors when he resorted to using cajolery and threats the other night, browbeating me into playing, and then —inducing me to take drugs!"

I got out my suitcase and started throwing things into it. I started throwing them harder and harder—then I threw the suitcase off the bed, scattering everything on the floor.

"Damn it! De Luna won't get off scot-free—I'll go back there and tell him exactly what I think of him."

PART FOUR
●
CODA

I.

The Vanishing Wizard

Early the next morning, after spending the night packing and putting my affairs in order, I gave notice to my landlord, climbed in my car and drove west, in the direction of the town in the mountains and don Diego's.

I arrived at the cabin around noon, walked to the door, tightened my fist, and rapped loudly. An echo—nothing else. Another knock—I pushed the door open and peeked inside. "Don Diego?" Cautiously, I entered. A minute later I emerged again, frustrated; he was not there.

"De Luna's probably up at the estate. Hmm. Well, going up the hill to find him is out of the question, isn't it, Alfonso? That is, unless you want to get lost, or maybe broken into little pieces by the watchpig —if not by the master himself."

With these thoughts to sober me, I decided to sit and wait for my former guitar teacher to show up. I was hungry so I went back into the cabin. In the kitchen I opened a tin box to find . . . biscuits. "What else?" I said. Then I spied the silver teapot again, and next to it, the bottle of wine I had brought don Diego as a gift.

"Now that would help the biscuits go down, wouldn't it," I thought. I found the corkscrew, unsentimentally drove it in, and un- stoppered the bottle. Then I went outside to the armchair and sat in the sun with my feet on the stump. After a gulp or two my patience was already wearing thin, so when I took another look at the mountain I made a decision—to go seek de Luna at the estate, and to hell with the consequences.

As I was about to replace the wine bottle on the shelf, curiosity prompted me to have a closer look at the silver teapot. I was about to put it back when a brilliant idea hit me—"Why not take the teapot along? . . ." If I was discovered by the master, I would simply explain that de Luna had asked me to return it to the house. Thin, but better than nothing. If it was stolen, as it might well be, de Luna would just have to deal with the consequences. Well, what of it? Hadn't he caused me a lot of trouble? He was just making trouble for himself. Didn't he have a long history of mucking with the possessions and rights of others? Like when he stole the cash from his father's cookie jar, and then the music book, too—not to mention pushing the Cigar of Power on me. ". . . It'll make a graphic exhibit when I tell him what I think of him."

I came out of the cabin door and walked around to the back, pausing a moment to consider the most likely spot to look for a path. But the forest at the edge of the clearing appeared to be a solid wall, and so I began to hike around the perimeter, searching for the inconspicuous breach I was sure must be there. Halfway around the circle I began to think the search was hopeless. That's when I looked down and saw the stub of one of don Diego's cigars. Playing a hunch, I thrust my arm into the vines—and grabbed hold of the mesh of a fishnet. I pulled it to the side, pushed a little more here and there, and found the borders of the curtain. I forced them apart and stepped through.

I found myself standing in an open chamber in the forest. A path began at my feet and led up the mountain through an arcade of trees which joined overhead in a fishbone configuration. Unlike the one from town to don Diego's, this path was not jammed by a claustrophobic tangle of greenery. No, indeed, this was an open corridor, a high-ceilinged, emerald chamber. There could be little doubt I had found the way to the estate.

This trail climbed at a faster rate than the other and was even divided into steps at points where it was necessary to mount the root system of a tree which had grown sideways from the slope. Because of the cathedral of trees I could not take references, but I reckoned I had entered one of the passes visible from don Diego's, taken a sharp right turn, and was now climbing sideways along the inner wall of the canyon.

I came to a small bridge over a stream fed by a delicate waterfall. The fall dropped in stages over the rocky cliffs whose tops were still far above me. I had a long ways to go, it seemed. And I was right—the hike continued for an hour, perhaps a little more. But at last I came to a steep, gracefully curved flight of stairs that led up to an archway of tree limbs framing only unobstructed blue sky.

I was feeling a great sense of anticipation when I came to the last six steps. I was close enough to the sky to almost touch it, yet the stairs were so steep I could see nothing over the top yet. As I climbed, the scene beyond came into view suddenly, which all the more heightened the drama of its unexpected grandeur. At the top I took a few paces forward and sat down on the hillside to take in the sweep of the landscape. The pride of it all was many miles in the distance, a range of majestic, snowcapped peaks stretching from one side of the horizon to the other—the northeastern spur of the Andes mountains. The sky was azure and heaped with clouds, some near and large, many others far away and small. Then came rippling folds of land, lush valleys, hills and mountains of misty blue and green. In the foreground, along the top of the crest, was the airstrip, a wide swath cut out of the forest with a grassy clearing maintained on either side. To the left was the long, undulating ridgeline of the mountain, parts of it still looming above eye level, twisted jungle trees clinging to the gray rock. And to the right, situated against a prominent gnarl in the mountain's spine and figuring as the crown jewel in the panorama of sights, was the estate house.

To describe what I saw as an estate or manor house is hopelessly inadequate, since it immediately suggests a cubic type of dwelling, however elaborate, laid out on level ground. This structure was neither.

First of all, it was staged on three staggered terraces rising up the knoll. The highest terrace was necessarily the smallest, and the lowest was the largest, comprising (from nearest to farthest) a strange pavilion of some sort, a long reflecting pool, and a courtyard backed by a wall at the foot of the second terrace. The first terrace was also the site of an opulent formal garden.

Secondly, none of the dominating structures was cubic. The forward pavilion was wedge-shaped, like a section of an amphitheatre. It was slightly below my eye level. Above eye level, on the third terrace, were two domes. And on the second terrace, about eye level, was a high, A-framed roof—the largest structure in the whole layout. To the left and right of the A-frame were other, lower roofs. Some were fairly conventional, others were shaped like pyramids and laid out in a saw-tooth design. The whole of it was well integrated into the landscape, flowing with the curves of the slope, preserving natural intrusions of rock and trees.

Most striking was the blackness of this vision. The bottom of the reflecting pool was black; so were the roofs of the A-frame and the pyramids. A black flange running the length of the courtyard wall separated into the two black railings on the stairway to the second terrace. But the two domes above and to the left of the main building were a translucent white—apparently frosted glass set in the geodesic framework.

"Those must be don Diego's greenhouses," I thought, rubbing my chin.

Even from that considerable distance there was a sense that the place was in a state of disrepair. It came as the sum of many minor flaws—the reflecting pool was empty and spotted with decayed vegetation and moss. Vines had taken over the wall at the rear of the courtyard, the garden hedges were uneven, flower beds were overgrown or, as it appeared, completely reclaimed by the forest.

The surrounding forest itself had a certain regularity of design as if it had once been an informal adjunct to those cultured hedges, trees, and flower banks near the pool.

My anger was now subdued beneath an intense curiosity. I looked around for the best approach to the estate house. The path was too obvious—it led straight down the hill and through the forest to the pavilion. The most promising route seemed to lie to my right, along the ridge to a point where the clearing ended and the wild forest joined the estate forest.

Soon I was slipping downhill between the trees toward the pool. Flashing glimpses of the pavilion came filtering through. Seen from the front, it too had a black surface, black as onyx.

I was cautiously approaching the sunlit border of the forest when to my left I heard an unmistakable sound. I froze in my tracks, snapping my head to the side. There he was, some twenty yards away, a hump-backed, porcine locomotive car, tossing his head, grunting, and sniffing the air. "The watchpig," I mouthed, breaking into a sweat.

It appeared his shoulder would reach my navel were we standing side by side—a relationship I had no wish to explore. His tiny eyes

167

were buried in fat and scar tissue. He looked like an uncompromisingly vicious sort of fellow, just as don Diego had described him.

"The watchpig," I whispered, and froze in my tracks.

The beast went back to rooting in the dirt. I took a step in reverse, moving as quietly as I could.

The watchpig abruptly stopped rooting and lifted his snout. He sniffed, snorted, and grunted. Then he took some zig-zagging, lunging steps in my direction.

"Oh my god, he's got my scent," I thought. "What am I going to do now?! I can't move or I'm a dead duck, but he'll be stepping on my toes in a minute. A-ha!"

I stooped over and grabbed the rock at my feet. Then I swung my arm back and let it fly over the watchpig's shoulder. He snorted and braced himself, then whirled around and charged after it like a bull rhino, crashing his ribs against tree trunks, squealing and grunting and frothing at the mouth as he regained his momentum and thundered on ahead. He overshot the mark and continued rampaging in circles, renewing his anger by crashing into trees.

Meanwhile, I took to my heels. I ran the length of the reflecting pool and hid near the edge of the courtyard. Now I had to stick close to the estate. In a minute the watchpig would give up and I couldn't risk him sniffing his way into my vicinity again. While I recovered my breath I had another look at the unswept courtyard and the general disrepair of the stonework. "Not much different from the cabin—the master really hired himself a gardener, didn't he." On the other hand, I thought, it was an enormous area for one old man to handle alone. I looked at the teapot and suddenly I was sorry I had brought it along. It was a miserable sort of trick I was contemplating—getting de Luna into trouble and perhaps costing him his job. He may have cost me a lot, but that was no reason to sink to the level of sly games myself. He was an old guy, and if he lost his job, then what would he do? Play guitar in town once a week for a living? Not likely. No, I had to ditch the silver teapot. Then I would circle to the rear of the house, to the frosty domes. De Luna was likely to be in there, if he was anywhere around this palace.

There was a planting urn on the courtyard floor not far from where I was hiding. It looked like a natural place to stash the teapot for an hour. I started to hop over the low wall but suddenly my arm was seized from behind in a grip that felt as if it would crush the bone. In a single motion I was jerked backward and spun around, and the teapot was wrested from my grasp.

The possessor of the hand with the steel grip was a huge, swarthy man with an anvil chin, tusky handlebar moustache and tiny, glowering eyes. His forehead was like a shot of tequila—two fingers high. He was wearing a gray jumpsuit and steel-toed work boots. On his belt he had a pistol in a black leather holster and a walkie-talkie. In short, he did not look like anyone I wanted to be on the wrong side of.

"What are you doing? Let me go!" I demanded.

He looked at the teapot and then at me with the contempt of a farmer for a weasel caught in a snare. "Why don't you settle down, boy, you're not going anywhere."

Keeping his eye on me, he pulled out his walkie-talkie and put a signal through. In a moment a voice crackled in his receiver.

"Yes?"

"Escovar, boss. I have a trespasser at the base of the steps."

"Got him?"

"Yeah. Looks like a thief, too."

"Everything under control?"

"Repeat, sir? Can't read you here."

"Is there any trouble?"

"No problem, sir."

"Bring him up to the house then, I'll meet you outside."

"Right."

He snapped the walkie-talkie back onto his belt.

"OK, fellow, let's go."

"Look, will you listen to me for just a second?"

"Yeah?"

"My name is Alfonso Fegoni. I'm a student, and I didn't steal that thing—I'm a friend of Diego de Luna's."

"So?"

"Don't you see? He borrowed it and I was just bringing it back for him."

"I don't know what you're trying to pull, boy, but I'm the chief of security here and I sure don't know no Diego de Luna."

"He's the gardener!"

"The gardener," he said drily. "OK, let's go."

The neanderthal started directing me by my elbow toward the stairs.

"Now wait a minute!"

"Look, kid . . ."

"Diego de Luna is the gardener here, he's been the gardener here for ten years at *least!*"

"It won't wash, kid. There's no regular gardener here—never has been. And I never heard of no Diego de Luna. Everybody who works here is on rotation—nobody ever stays for more than three months at a time. Nobody could have been here for even one year, let alone ten."

"No, you're wrong, you must be wrong."

"Well, why don't you tell the boss about it, then—all right? Now come along. Just be cooperative and you won't get hurt."

Thus dismayed and bewildered I was escorted up the stairs toward the front of the great A-framed building. When we were within a stone's throw, a door opened and a familiar figure stepped out. He was wearing a T-shirt, pants with suspenders, and a pair of weathered old boots. He was also smoking a cigar.

"You see? There he is now," I said. "Don Diego!"

De Luna had on his sunglasses. He looked in our direction, but nothing registered in his expression.

"Here he is Boss," said Escovar. "Caught him red-handed trying to hide this teapot."

My eyes must have showed white all around as the identity of Diego de Luna, gardener and guitar player, crumbled before me, leaving standing in his place—who?

De Luna approached us frowning and puffing his cigar.

"Escovar, you are an incompetent."

I thought that unfair. "Don Diego, you shouldn't blame . . ."

"How did this jackal get in here in the first place without electronic surveillance picking him up?!"

My mouth dropped open.

"Sir, electronic surveillance was down for an hour today. He must have slipped in then."

"It goes to show you, doesn't it? Let down your guard for one second, and the place is overrun with poachers, trespassers, and thieves. Why was the E.S. system down, anyway?"

"One of the elements burned. It took a while to test out."

"Well—why didn't you have a backup system in place?"

"Don Diego . . ."

"Speak when you're spoken to, kid!" said Escovar. "I didn't have a backup because when I requested one last month you told me it was too expensive and I should wait until the new year."

"Oh yes, ahem, so I did, so I did. Well, then I take back what I said about your being incompetent. You were very alert, very alert."

"What shall I do with him, boss?"

"Do with him? Hmm, seems to me I've seen this one lurking around here before."

"You have, sir?"

"Yes, and I believe I warned him personally to keep his tail off the premises."

"He must have broke in to get the teapot, sir."

"Right you are."

"Should I take him to the district police?"

"No, I think not."

"No?"

"There's far too much lenience in law enforcement these days. I think we should teach him a lesson he'll never forget."

"Oh come on!" I pleaded.

"What do you want to do, sir?"

"I think fifteen lashes would do the job, Escovar," said don Diego and he turned to leave.

"Don Diego!"

"Sir, are you sure . . . ?"

"You think that's too severe? Well, perhaps you're right. Why don't you leave him here and we'll discuss the matter in the cold clear light of reason."

"Sir?"

"Go on, Escovar, I'll take over from here on."

"Should I stay nearby, sir?"

"Why don't you get on the transmitter and order that backup surveillance system. Obviously we need it if we're to prevent this kind of thing from happening in the future."

"Yes sir," muttered the bewildered Escovar as he walked away. "Uh, what about this?" he asked, remembering the teapot.

"With the rest of the silver, in the vault."

When Escovar was gone, don Diego said in a mildly accented English, "Well, young man, what do you think is an appropriate penalty in the face of this trespassing, this invasion of my privacy—not to mention the theft of my silver?" He laughed aloud and crossed his arms over his chest.

"It's not funny."

"If you could have seen the look on your face when Escovar called me 'boss,' you'd think it was funny, too. Do you like it, Alfonso—the grounds, I mean?" Don Diego waved a hand in the air. "Almost completely self-sufficient. Everything is solar. The big roof, those pyramids over there contribute; the pool and the obelisk used to be part of it, but we cut those out a few years ago—didn't need them—only a few people here at any one time anymore . . . say, Alfonso, you're not mad, are you?"

"Now I see why you didn't want Melinda to come and research you."

"Why's that?"

"You didn't want to be exposed!"

"That's right, I already know enough people. I don't need to know any more. I don't need more people, I need peace of mind! And that means doing what I want to do, and being left alone to do it."

"You tricked me, that's the way I see it—you tricked me right down the line, don Diego—or whatever your name is. And now you can stand there and laugh at your one-sided joke. Does it make you feel clever, pulling Alfonso's strings, and pushing Alfonso's buttons?"

"But no, my friend! I am sorry to hear that you feel so betrayed— but it is only the untimeliness of your discovery that gives that impression. If it had happened in due course, it would have amused you, too. I did not trick you—I *am* Diego de Luna! Now why don't we both sit down over here, and I will give you a full explanation."

I wordlessly followed him to a nearby crescent-shaped stone bench. We sat down at opposite ends of it. In the shade de Luna removed his sunglasses and I stared off at a diagonal as he began to talk.

"Let me take you back a few years, Alfonso. When I was about thirty, I had already been performing under the name Diego de Luna for a good decade. Diego de Luna—after the moon in my dream. Yes, I had the vision I spoke of when I was only twenty. Though I had no idea at the time what the dream meant, it was simply another one of those remarkable and unusual events I thought set me apart and made me something special. During those years—some of the best of my life —I played the guitar religiously, with a passion. I fed all the raw energy of my youth into the guitar. You can see why, can't you? . . . No? It glorified the most marvelous event in the universe! I speak of myself, of course. And I, myself, was devoted to music, so it was a mutual glorification."

"But what about all this? Did you inherit a fortune, or what?"

"Inherit? No, I earned this house and this land."

"Playing guitar?!"

"Give me time, lad, to come to the point. Everything I said about my origins is true. But at thirty, the story takes another course. Diego de Luna was going strong when I was thirty, but he was fading fast by the time I was thirty-one. That's when I began to build . . ." he waved his hand, "my empire, you might say."

"You mean you stopped playing guitar? Why?"

"I stopped being Diego de Luna. I had no time for it. The owner of the restaurant where I was working as a waiter offered to sell me his part of the business for a pittance, and I leaped at the opportunity. He gave it to me cheap because he liked me and knew of my financial problems and because, well, because he was dying and had no relations. It was also because he liked my guitar playing, he said—which is a twist of fate, for my guitar playing began to wane as a result of his kindness." Don Diego shrugged his shoulders.

"You were working as a waiter? Why?"

"Music was too unsteady, Alfonso. Too unsteady and there wasn't enough money in it for a man with a growing family. I had to take another job and waiting tables was about all I could do. Guitar players, even good ones, didn't earn much in those days, Alfonso—how many of them do now? And as you can probably tell, my singing didn't win any prizes either. I was moderately successful for a while, it is true. But success boxes you in, like a job. There was heavy pressure to become a formula player. You can wreck yourself by being an experimenter once you're established. By the time I was thirty I was bored with listening to myself, my audience was happy but not expanding, and it was clear I would be doing the same exact thing ten years later."

"But you could have gone into teaching, couldn't you?"

"No credentials, Alfonso, and urgent needs in the immediate present. But yes, I did try teaching private lessons. Then I found myself subject to the whims of a bunch of dilettantes. It was enough to destroy the love of the guitar to pour one's efforts into a sieve like that. That was just what was eating me more and more, my friend, seeing my best efforts being poured through a sieve. I played to reach people's hearts, but I got the idea I was just aiding their digestion most of the time—that or boosting trade at the bar. Meanwhile, I was being bullied about by the material, practical world.

"Having a family to support made all the difference. In my youth I disdained practical realities in favor of art, beauty, poetry, adventuring and excitement, but I found myself subject to the lordship of material necessity all the same in the end. The hard facts have the rudest way of making themselves felt. Try to picture yourself waiting tables the rest of your life, for example—if you can. That's what I had to look forward to. Also try to imagine your wife, who loved your guitar playing once upon a time, interrupting you in the middle of a song to say, 'Have we paid the back rent yet? What about the new furniture you promised? You don't pay enough attention to me,' and the like of that.

"I was very oppressed, Alfonso, and I saw money as a way out— the only way out. In fact, after getting a taste of it, I was determined to be not just comfortable, but rich, filthy, dirty rich. And that's when I broke with the guitar, when I started off on this new quest, or obsession, if you prefer."

"Maybe if you'd just had a good job, you wouldn't have gone to such an extreme."

"Good job? Almost a contradiction in terms. I needed risk, and adventure—not so-called security. It was security, that is to say routine and stagnation, that was driving me crazy. Besides, Alfonso, I've known all my life just what I wanted to do, and it never had the least correspondence with what anybody else wanted me to do. What else besides economic independence would do for such a person?"

"Nothing, I guess. What did you do, open a chain of restaurants?"

Don Diego laughed. "No, Alfonso. No, twenty-five years ago it was possible to get in on the ground floor of the oil business here, and you know where it's gone since then." He scratched the back of his head. "Then, I kept diversifying. I've played my hunches, and with remarkable success, if I do say so myself." He looked at his fingernails and then smiled at me jokingly.

"Coffee?"

"Coffee, yes, sure. But now let me finish up my story, eh? I'll show you what sort of businesses I have a hand in later."

"OK. But can I ask a question?"

"Yes?"

"Was that thing about a spiritual center the truth?"

"Oh yes. I did fictionalize my role as de Luna—but that's pardonable, for he was my shadow, and had actually been stalking me through all the years since I let him wither from substance."

"Your shadow?"

"Yes, Alfonso. I not only had trouble finding time to play my guitar as I became more involved with business affairs, but I also abandoned it with my heart. There was something incompatible about the two ways of life, for one thing. For another, I was disillusioned. I've told you some of the reasons why."

"But why were the two ways of life incompatible?"

"That is a tough question, Alfonso. To some people I suppose they are not. But I found my old sense of values just did not apply in the new climate. And in a way, the guitar represented those values.

"You see, I started out feeling superior to other people playing the empire-building game. But I found my wisdom was virtually irrelevant. I had to begin to think like them in order to survive. I was forced to become obsessed with the balance sheet and nothing but the balance sheet. Continually I had to ask what was in it for me, or my business, or the people to whom I owed favors. People will always profess to be virtuous, even those who are ruthlessly grasping for power, so I had to learn to dissemble myself and to distrust people's motives routinely; and I'll tell you—they had to distrust me sometimes, and not without reason."

"That sounds awfully cynical."

"It's what is, that's all. But you have it—I had become awfully cynical by the age of fifty-five. Worldly, if you care to put it politely. Guitar?" He laughed. "Part of the naive world of children. The sight of it didn't make me nostalgic, it made me bitter. How could I sing about magic, miracles, the power of love, the everlasting bliss found in a woman's arms, the plight of the downtrodden, the world of peace that would dawn if only people would love one another and recognize our universal brotherhood?"

Don Diego raised his hands, made a wry face, and then let them drop in his lap.

"But now you say you are Diego de Luna."

"Now I am."

"But how? What do you mean when you say that?"

"Well, I take you back to the spiritual center. There was the projection in concrete terms of my shadow. It was an effort to rejuvenate the part of my soul I thought I had lost over the years. As I told you, I even thought that with my financial power we could fire up a beacon here that would spread light throughout the world. When I discovered the same rot infecting my crystal palace as infected the world at large, it was the last straw. I said, 'The human race be damned!' Life had no thrill and no wonder in it after that, none."

He was silent a second, then he began again.

"What I said about the old badger cutting himself off from the world is absolutely true. I tore up the road, threw everyone out, started conducting as much of my business as possible from here. I had built the place as a retreat in the first place, that's why all the solar equipment, and the greenhouse gardens."

"At least you still enjoyed making money."

"Money-making had lost its savor, too. I had more than I could possibly need. My time was mainly spent in holding on to it. I was a slave to it, in a sense. As I sat up here on this mountain listening to records, reading books, or plunking my old guitar, I wondered what there was left to do, except perhaps shoot myself."

"Why didn't you?"

"Shoot myself?"

"Yeah."

"And mar this pretty face? No, I wouldn't have done that."

"Was there a flash of light then, and you saw that being de Luna was what you were meant to be?"

Don Diego laughed. "No, it wasn't like that."

"How then?"

"It so happened that I ran out of fertilizer for my gardens one week —oh, six months or so after the end of the spiritual center. It seemed like a ridiculous waste of money to hire a plane to fly in a hundred pounds of, if you'll pardon the expression, bullshit, when I could just as easily hike on into town and get it myself. Besides, I'd sequestered myself here for six months with next to nothing to do, and I was getting a little itchy. But I decided not to attract attention by coming on as the *patrón*, the master, the man of money. So I went down dressed in my work clothes, covered with dirt, unshaven, hair grown out long. And I went up to the grain and feed store and said I was the gardener for the estate on the mountain, and I needed a hundred pounds of fertilizer. And do you know, they treated me very well. The shopkeeper asked me my name and on the spur of the moment I said, Diego de Luna. When he saw that I was on foot, he had his son help me carry the stuff up the mountain. We took it as far as the cabin, and I made two trips that afternoon to take it the rest of the way up.

"After that, Alfonso, I began to go down and visit regularly. I made a lot of good friends, and I started bringing my guitar down to entertain. And that's how Diego de Luna came to be reborn—little by little. At first it was a bit like play-acting, but then it became much more. My sense of humor was restored, my sense of life's magic, too. I played the guitar as I had always wanted to play it, as a free extension of my heart, for no particular reward. It was like a rebirth for me.

"But I hasten to point out I could not have done it by playing the part to a mirror. I did it because my friends found it in me."

"How was that?"

"Confronted with these fine people, my loyal friends, whose sincerity I could not doubt, who sought not to exploit me in any way, my cynicism had nothing to grasp hold of.

"But it hardly seemed reasonable to believe I had found the only sincere, good people on the face of the earth right here in my own town. That's when I came up with an answer that satisfied me, and put my mind at ease."

"What was that?"

"The Flies In Marmalade Theory."

"What?"

"Yes. Basically I think we are all more or less spiritual beings— otherwise why would we all understand and respond to music, eh? Yes, we are all spiritual, all alike under the skin. But we must live in this world and survive. We've got to eat, so we go after the marmalade.

And when we go down in the jar, we get stuck in it like buzzing little flies, wiggling in the goop. Society is a great impersonal marmalade, and all our feet are stuck in it. We are all such busy, driven little flies we can easily forget there are other things. There's no way to avoid being a little fly, and leading a life dependent on marmalade, but it's up to a few who remember to remind the others of beauty, of mystery, and of spirit, for without these things I believe we would indeed live the lives of insects. Now you can suggest such intangibles to people with words, Alfonso, but with music you can tickle the very fibers of a person's soul; with music people are at but one remove from the source. Music is moonlight, Alfonso, reflected sun. That is why music is so important. That is why you cannot imagine a world without music."

"You have helped me see more value in music than I ever suspected was there, don Diego."

"Thank you, Alfonso. That shows a change in you, you know. You didn't seem to find much that was meaningful in art, as though it was only a kid's game."

"I . . . I guess I don't think that anymore."

"I hope you'll forgive me for deceiving you, Alfonso, but I wanted to preserve my identity until I was absolutely certain I could trust you not to leak the word to anyone. Including Escovar—you see? I am fond of my life the way it is, and I want to pass the rest of it without change. More than that, my identity was a scratch glass to see whether you were diamond or paste."

"One thing I don't get, don Diego."

"Yes?"

"If you see yourself as a cultivator of spirits, and music is your medium, why didn't you open a guitar school and get a whole lot more of your work done? Why don't you make this place a retreat for musicians, even?"

Don Diego smiled.

"Well, apart from the complications that would arise, Alfonso, that's just not the way, it wouldn't work. Haven't you seen my teaching methods? Not only would I not have any fun at it, but there's a basic contradiction between formal, organized instruction and what I do.

"You see, there is another lesson I took from my experience with life, and the gurus in particular: Every time a man sets out to organize, he invokes the marmalade. Therefore, I have decided to entrust my fate to the same forces that brought me my vision. Think of it! It took me thirty years to appreciate the point of a single encounter with them! How could I dare presume to take the reins from such intelligence? No, now I relax and let them use me to fulfill their purposes. I look for clues as to how I am to assist in daily life, and am richly rewarded."

"How do you know when what you're looking at is a clue, though?"

Don Diego raised his index finger. "By the advent of the meaningful coincidence!"

"What is a meaningful coincidence?"

"A law operates in the universe, Alfonso, bringing about the most unlikely occurrences between intelligent beings. This is because all the universe is interconnected, the smallest contains the largest, and vice versa—matter and mind and spirit are intertwined. The moments when reality behaves like magic or like dream—that's when we know."

"We know?"

"We know! For example, if I had gone out and set up my guitar school, you would have been the last person in the world to come in and sign up for lessons. When you found me, you were on a search, and that's why you found me. If you had signed up for guitar lessons, it would have been an 'intellectually stimulating experience' for you at best. Marmalade, marmalade. You can call it luck that you stumbled across my path, but I don't. Consider your vision, or dream, I guess you'd call it—too much to be a simple coincidence—it was a cosmically synchronous event!"

"You mean, you think I was literally guided to you by spirits, don Diego?"

"No, I don't say they guided you here. They probably found you wandering around like a lost sheep and whispered something in your ear to help you find your way. But you've made all the decisions, to take or not to take this opportunity or that one. Look at me, I ignored my dream for thirty years—I had to try all the dead ends."

Now, I thought, I understood things much better. My first impression of don Diego was basically right—he *had* wanted to induct me into his delusionary world, a world of divine coincidences, spirit, karma, and guitar. But now I also saw that he had acted in good faith —unselfishly, in a strange sense—like a latter-day Pied Piper. He reminded me of a lot of old men who dream big dreams and talk a grandiose line when they have become no longer effectual in the world, and it is hard to be angry with such people. Then, too, don Diego was an exception to this portrait in so many ways, and such an intense person, I considered myself lucky to have known such a remarkable fellow.

All the same, I knew I had to leave the guitar apprenticeship, even if it weren't for having to leave Venezuela. I didn't like the idea of this imperious old mystic discovering the design of my life for me, and then doing his best to make sure I conformed to the script. But most of all, I was still mad, mad because I'd traded my career for a bunch of guitar tricks—and if not for his influence it would never have happened. Not to mention the Cigar of Power.

"Well, Alfonso, I have done an awful lot of talking. Now it is your turn to speak your mind."

"I don't know what to say, my head is still spinning."

"Well, why don't you tell me why you've come all the way back here today? It must be something important."

"Oh, uh, no, it's not really important . . . I . . . I only had one class today, in the morning, and it ended early. So I thought I'd take a drive, you know, and prolong the weekend spirit."

"That's good."

"And, just on a whim, I guess, I came back here."

"On a whim? That doesn't sound like you."

"No, uh, I guess it doesn't. What I was really . . . uh, really hoping was that you could . . . get me another Cigar of Power."

At this don Diego burst out laughing. "Sure, Alfonso," he said, slapping his knee, "I have a whole box of them inside the house."

"A whole box? But you said . . ."

"That cigar didn't have any mixture of herbs and plant extracts in it!"

"No?"

"No! It was a perfectly ordinary cigar. Well, I wouldn't go so far as to say that—they're actually the best I have, a handmade Cuban import, which is probably why you've never seen one before."

"Then . . . then how did it do what it did to my ears? How did it . . ."

"That was you—you, Alfonso!" don Diego beamed. "The cigar just tricked your self-imposed barriers into withdrawing and you did what you did because you believed you could do it. You succeeded brilliantly, as long as you could give the responsibility for your success over to the Cigar of Power. But in fact it was your spirit, and your faith, my friend, pure and simple."

"Well . . . I'll be darned."

Following that, don Diego showed me around the estate house. What I could say about the tour would certainly add to the story of Diego de Luna, but not to the story we are here to tell.

Later, when don Diego and I were walking down the steps toward the reflecting pool, he asked me why I had brought the teapot, and I told him the truth (but not the whole truth), that is, that I had brought it to claim as an excuse for my being there in case I was caught. De Luna found that an amusing case of short-sightedness on my part. Then he said he admired my guts, considering what he had told me about the watchpig and the master.

"Well, Alfonso, shall I accompany you back down the mountain?"

"What about the jaguar? Do you think you ought to bring your gun?"

"No, that jaguar must have moved on. No sign of him for quite a while."

"Well then, I guess I'll hoof it alone, don Diego. No sense in putting yourself out."

"It's no trouble."

"I'd just rather go it alone."

Don Diego stopped with his hands behind his back. He put his chin down against his neck and, after considering his thoughts for a second, he said, "You're not still mad about Sunday, are you?"

"Mad?"

"Yes, I guess you didn't get much sleep that night, what with your leaving so late, and class the next day."

"Oh. Yeah, but that's OK."

"Well, I don't blame you for getting peeved at me—but look what you got out of staying, eh? Ten years from now, which is going to be more memorable—that Monday at school, or your night at La Fortuna?"

Don Diego shook my hand. "See you next week, eh?"

"Uh, right!" I said, thinking of a letter I would write to explain why I had to leave. I was too upset at the moment to deal with it any other way. Indeed, what I wanted most was to get away from this strange country, and go to a peaceful place—a place like my own bedroom back in the States, there to lie on my bed and stare up at the ceiling, a glass of milk and some homemade oatmeal cookies within arm's reach, the radio tuned to a station which played instrumental retakes of last year's pop tunes.

177

"Say, what about the watchpig?" I remembered.

"The watchpig, eh?"

"Yeah, what if he takes after me on the way out of here?"

"Trivial, trivial—he's very responsive to his name. If he comes after you, simply yell, 'Yankee! Go home!' "

Don Diego winked, turned around and began hiking spryly back toward the main house.

II.

The Path of the Jaguar

The flight was a long one. Or so it seemed, until the pilot signaled the start of our descent toward Los Angeles International. I pressed my face to the window, watching the familiar brown mountains and murky yellow air rising closer by degrees to the gray metal wing. Though one could not point with pride to these things while, say, taking a visitor from space on a tour, the sight of the freeway interchanges and the myriad aqua-bottomed swimming pools (among other things) was somehow welcome and reassuring.

On the ride home with my folks I generally turned aside questions, responding with as few words as possible. They knew very little as yet —nothing about Diego de Luna, and not much more about Dr. Forzosa. The atmosphere was charged with anticipation over the forthcoming explanation of my washout, but they kept it all politely restrained. I was not up to full explanations yet. I was deeply exhausted by the events of the previous two weeks and needed at least a day's rest before revealing just how I had traded a college career for a half-dozen guitar lessons. "Didn't even get Britt's address," I thought one more time, and sighed.

My youngest sister, Rita, was along too, and it was clear from her interest in the passing scenery and attempts to sponsor other topics of conversation that she would much rather have been elsewhere—a sentiment with which I had considerable sympathy.

When we pulled up to our pleasant, modest suburban dwelling and my father set the emergency brake, I wondered what all the homesickness had been for—nothing had changed. The street was flat and straight, the sidewalk was cracked in the same old places, the lawn was neatly trimmed, as it always had been. Inside, the familiar odors of the living room and kitchen brought on a feeling of safety and security that was at once reassuring and oppressive. It would be two weeks at the limit before I was engaging in the same tired old quarrels and feeling like a captive in my own house. All this I had bought for myself, too.

"Mom, Dad, if you don't mind, I think I'll go upstairs and take a nap. I'm still running on Venezuelan time, you know."

"You should get some sleep, Alfonso," said my mom. "You look so pale. I'll fix you a nice dinner, and wake you up when it's ready."

Several times already I had heard how much thinner I looked.

I passed the living room on my way to the stairs. Rita was sitting cross-legged on the rug with the telephone to her ear. She waved at me. I had two suitcases in my hands, so I just smiled. She covered the receiver with her other hand.

"Hey, where's your guitar, anyway, Al?"

"I sold it."

"What?! What didja do that for?"

"That . . . is a long story," I replied as I began trudging up the staircase.

I came into my bedroom, dropped the suitcases by the bed and walked around to the window. The sun had set but the sky still glowed a pale, deepening blue.

I turned and, heaving a sigh, let myself fall straight across the bed. After the weeks of city noises in my Caracas apartment, the jet flight, and the havoc normal to an airline terminal, the silence that filled my ears was akin to a refreshing draught from a mountain stream.

Then I thought how I had not rinsed the taste of smoke-flavored almonds out of my mouth and how thirsty I was besides. I tried to move my body, but my body was not ready to move. My limbs were like sandbags, the deep breaths I took sounded like sleep itself was already upon me. But I knew I was awake, wide awake inside, and my mind held fast to the image and sensation of the cooling, rushing water I would find in the bathroom if I would just rise up out of this black well of friendly, care-obliterating sleep into which I was sinking. I lay there making up my mind while the room went dark with night.

"All right, all right," I said to myself, rolling off the bed and staggering to the bathroom. Without even bothering to turn on the light, I went to the sink and ducked my head under the faucet with my eyes closed.

Then it was on my cheek, the splashing, gurgling water, and I was sucking in great mouthfuls and gulping them down. Finally I was satisfied, and I pushed myself away with my palms and looked at the shimmering ribbon of crystalline liquid that fell down the face of a huge stone slab the color of blue steel. "What's this, a waterfall?" I thought. "A waterfall!"

On the stone, and all around me, I sensed, was a soft silvery light. I tilted my head back and the high, full moon seemed to acknowledge my glance with its benignant smile.

I backed off a step from the stone slab and, incredulously, began to look things over. The fall from which I had been drinking came from a spring whose waters ran in a stair-step fashion down the face of a cliff. Isolated trees of a peculiar shape grew between the rocks. The water ran past my feet, fanned out over a bank of pebbles, and then flowed gently into a shallow, glassy stream with many rounded stones protruding above the waterline. Beyond the moonlit stream was a path into a forest, and on the path, staring at me over his shoulder, was . . . the jaguar. Under the moonlight his coat was platinum, and a faint silver haze surrounded his body.

It was strange to know I was dreaming, and yet, at the same time to be so acutely conscious—aware of myself and an infinite number of details composing the scene. It was more real than real, and I felt more myself than myself. I would not have thought of pinching my arm, or wiping my eyes—I did not question such potency.

The jaguar exerted a magnetic attraction on my gaze, and there was a determination on my part to hold him in view, so that he did not slip away like a mirage and leave me with the mystery of his nature unresolved.

I spoke to him in a plain, clear voice. "Are you dream being? Are you spirit guide?" He wavered slightly, his paw raised as if he were halted on the verge of moving ahead. "What are you here for, then?" I asked, knowing as the words left my mouth that I should have put it the other way around.

At this he put his paw down and paced forward a couple of steps. He looked back once and then began trotting up the trail in the same direction he had been facing to begin with.

Without hesitation I skipped down the bank to the stream and began hopping from stone to stone. It never occurred to me to be afraid. Indeed I was urged forward by a desire to settle the enigma posed by this disturbing, silent phantom once and for all.

Turning leftward, the jaguar passed out of sight behind a boulder. When I reached the same turn I looked upward at a trail which climbed steeply through a cleft in two massive rocks and then went to the left again around the side of a vertical cliff.

As I raced up the path between the rocks they seemed to grow in height and when I made the turn I found I was high on the sheer face of a mountain. Such are the peculiarities of dreams, one thing joining another in a way that seems sensible at the time, but quite impossible upon later reflection.

There were no trees here, only rocks and boulders and the massive face of the mountain itself. I heard a strong wind blowing, but felt only a breeze on my face and arms. The sound seemed to be above us as yet, up where the gunmetal blue side of the escarpment rose against the sky and the moonlit details of its surface dwindled into imperceivable, glimmering specks with the distance.

The jaguar was well ahead of me, far higher and climbing with sure-footed grace. I started jogging and I moved with light steps, as if gravity were greatly reduced. Mere running felt like dancing. With no perceptible effort, every step was gliding me forward another ten feet. Yet the distance between us was not diminishing quickly.

There were more turns in the trail ahead as the mountain face curved and folded like a gigantic drapery. I looked to the right, into the chasm, and saw impossible rocky spires growing out of a boundless pool of blue-black space. They were capped in a shimmering iridescence, an almost liquid intensification of the moonlight.

Sometimes the trail cut into a fold, or ran between a cleft in the rocks, only to emerge again, clinging to the sheer face of the mountain. But no matter how unreasonably the trail turned, the celestial orb remained fixed in the same general location, as if no turn had been made at all.

The higher we climbed, the more the sound of the wind increased. Gusts swept over the trail now, sometimes catching me full in the face and whipping my hair about. But I could sense such gusts whether they touched me or not. Sometimes several enormous, turbulent dervishes, as large as houses, would go hurtling past and roar off over the indigo void like invisible genies who had never yet known the prison of a magic lamp.

Now the chase seemed to be reaching some kind of climax. I had been gaining on the jaguar, and we were nearing the black edge of the mountain top. The trail had gotten narrower. I looked on my right and the tops of the spires were far below. Further on was an endless expanse of inky darkness with weirdly shaped geo-forms bulging out of the depths. It was like looking into an ocean where light barely penetrated and shapes were descried by their own dull phosphorescence. At a height far above a natural horizon, moonglow sky gradually merged with the sooty blue murkiness.

There was a monolithic ledge of overhanging rock ahead. Underneath, a cave ran a good sixty yards. The trail took a steep turn on the far side of this overhang and then doubled back. I was almost on the heels of the jaguar when he bounded up the lift in the trail, cut across to the back of the rocks and disappeared overhead.

The gap in time between the jaguar's leap and my arrival on the top of the slab of overhanging rock must have been only seconds. But when I pulled myself upright at the top of the climb and looked ahead, I knew the chase was over. It was over and I had lost.

I was staring into a blind canyon. It was fully illuminated by the moon and I could see there was no exit except over the rock on which I stood. The jaguar was gone, vanished into the vertical walls some one hundred feet high.

While I walked disconsolately forward, the wind played games overhead, pinwheel currents rolling by, long, sheet-like gusts touching down against the rocks at the top of the canyon, making the cracks, crevices, and jagged edges sing. But it could not descend into the narrow gap between the sheer walls, and the oddly shaped pool of water at the end of the canyon was as smooth as a mirror. About thirty feet long, and shaped roughly like a corseted circle, it was fed by a slender ribbon of water which fell from the top of the far wall to the rock-bed floor of the canyon in a noiseless, clinging stream.

As I went, I picked up rocks and tossed them down again to clatter over other lifeless rocks. The moon reflecting in the pool caught my attention. The image had a razor-edged precision that was quite uncanny. It moved away from me as I approached the pool edge, finally settling at the center when I stopped walking.

With one last pebble in my hand I stood and observed the smiling face. The desolate surroundings seemed to capture my feeling in their very appearance, for here I was, drawn to the outermost limit of a barren wilderness, chasing a nameless phantom who evaporated and left me with nothing but worthless rocks and silent shadows for all my travail. In just such a way had de Luna enticed me into chasing after a phantom world he had concocted out of his beliefs—the domain of guitar knowledge, and all its precious gems—until the real world I'd neglected rolled on over me. I woke up too late then, and here I was, dreaming again. I wanted to put an end to this one now. "What am I to learn by this?" I said bitterly, and impulsively pitched the small stone I held into that imperturbably joyful Buddha at the center of the pool.

I turned my head in the violence of the motion, but to my surprise, I heard no splash, no breaking of the surface. Instead I heard the wind cease, and coming back from the pool, the sound of a silver chime. And then another chime came from deeper below the surface, the tones of the two overlapping. Then came another, and another, each time deeper, until layers and layers of vibration resounded upward to the surface, rising all the way from the bottom of the blue-black sea I had climbed above.

The shattered moonlight spread across the surface of the pool and covered it with fragments of silver light. But these fragments did not move like ordinary, random reflections—they moved like living creatures. They effervesced vigorously, and as they did so they caught the raw vibration funneling upward from deep down below and converted it into . . . music. How else can I describe what I was seeing, for the fragments sang like instruments as they glistered and wavered, yet their instrumental voices spoke like words.

I was captivated instantly by what I saw—indeed I do not think I could have looked away if I had wanted to. I took a step closer, and the sound reached out to me, the hypnotic fascination deepened. The luminous flecks were playing a tantalizing game, always seeming to dart away just as my gaze was about to penetrate the whole meaning of their melody. Each one I watched and listened to somehow brought me physically closer to all of them. As I drifted nearer I seemed to be becoming weightless, losing my body. They were drawing me in, out of myself and into the pool, among the coruscating patterns of light and music.

But I did not care, I knew I was coming closer to understanding what was meant by the melodies, the songs within the lights that swam like schools of fishes in geometric arrays. Now I could almost run my hand through them, touch them and feel the personality of each—every shade of emotion, pleasure, pain, joy, sorrow, desire. . . . But then they began to change, growing more complex and subtle. Where there had been tunes and airs there were now symphonies and fugues, liquid architectures of sound, shifting forms of awesome intricacy and beauty.

All the while the fundamental vibration had been growing. The lights, the sounds, were not only streaming and harmonizing in more complex shapes and structures, they were becoming brighter, more dazzling to behold. Then the teeming lights began to fuse together—there were already patches too intense to look into directly. The sound too was swelling, melding into a vast chorus where no voice was distinct, like the roar of waves magnified many times and extended through all space.

Then, in the midst of all this intense, shimmering beauty, I felt a slight tremor of fear, and with that I began to lose the vision, and consciousness itself. The great chorus of voices suddenly grew quiet, the lights began to diffuse, soften and disperse. I had the sensation of being adrift, floating in a pale gray ocean. And with the floating came a deep calmness, and sleep.

My eyes fluttered open. For a moment I wasn't sure where I was, until I focused on my bedstead, desk, chair, and wall posters. I let out a little laugh. I was home, in my room! Everything was OK . . . very OK . . . extremely ecstatically superordinarily OK!

I rolled over and looked out the window. Night had fallen. I jumped up, lifted the window sash and poked my head out. There was no moon in the sky, none. There was, however, a big green-white street lamp staring back at me. This made me laugh some more.

I felt as if a fever had broken. Indeed my forehead was soaked in a cool sweat. I was so glad to be alive that I felt like literally kissing the earth. My problems, the obsessions of the last two weeks, seemed so very distant at that moment that they might as well have belonged to somebody else—a guy living around the corner—the fellow that used to live here until an hour ago.

"This can't last," I told myself soberly. "But it can!" I thought. "Dear don Diego . . . dear don Diego! I've got to write to him. Now! I've got to write now while it's still fresh. But where am I going to write to? He doesn't have an address—hell, I don't know . . . c/o the Rincon Café, or was it Restaurant? Write it down, write it down! Don't forget it . . . don't."

I turned toward the darkened room. My eyes were adjusted to the street lamp, and stepping forward in the darkness I stubbed my toe on the leg of the bed.

"Ow! Ow! Ow!" I whispered, "Keep it quiet!" and cursing, I made my way by touch to the desk, where I proceeded to pull a little over-zealously on the top drawer, jamming it sideways. I yanked it hard and it unfroze suddenly, causing my hand to jerk out and slam into the back of the chair, rapping my knuckles as the contents of the drawer went crashing to the floor.

I shouted a four-letter expletive and shook my hand. Then I heard my mother's footsteps down below. I counted them—one, two, three. She stopped at the foot of the stairs.

"Alfonso? Are you all right?"

I went to my door, opened it and leaned out.

"Yeah, ma, I'm *all right.*"

"What happened?"

"Nothing."

"Hey Al!" Rita shouted out.

"Hey what?!"

"Melinda called," she said with drippy sweetness.

"And?"

"She wants you to call her back. She said she has two tickets for a guitar concert and she's looking forward to seeing you."

"Oh yeah? Well, well." I smiled. "I'm looking forward to seeing her, too."

"Who's Melinda, Al?" said my sis.

"She's almost as much trouble as you, that's who she is."

Appendix A

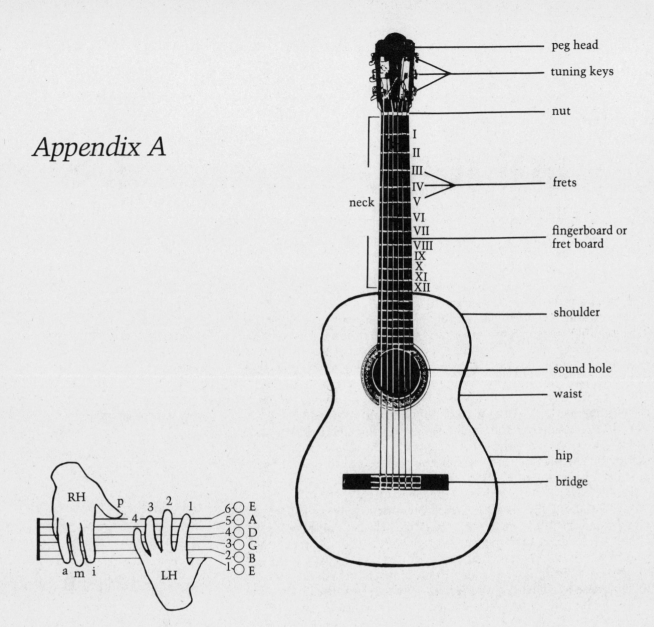

peg head
tuning keys
nut
frets
fingerboard or
fret board
shoulder
sound hole
waist
hip
bridge

neck

I
II
III
IV
V
VI
VII
VIII
IX
X
XI
XII

RH

p   3 2   1
     4

6 ○ E
5 ○ A
4 ○ D
3 ○ G
2 ○ B
1 ○ E

a m i

LH

On Tuning the Guitar

Musicians could not play with one another if there were no agreed-upon standard for the pitches of the notes. Such a standard has evolved over time and it is important for you to get in the habit of using it early in your guitar career, not only for this reason but because your instrument was designed with standard pitch in mind (too much tension can be harmful, too little sounds dull).

Tuning can be difficult at first, but it gets easier as your ear gets more sensitive, and a tuned-in ear is undeniably an asset for any musician. Playing on a poorly tuned instrument is psychologically debilitating since it's a problem no amount of technique can overcome. So, to work at tuning skill is as vital and rewarding as any other aspect of guitar playing.

Some rare individuals are blessed with a perfect memory for pitch. Their gift is called *absolute pitch* or *perfect pitch*. The rest of us, however, must rely on a tuning instrument. Each string may be tuned separately to a standard pitch if you possess six tuning forks—or better yet, a guitarist's pitch pipe or a piano.

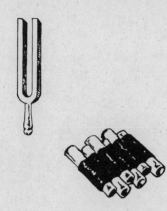

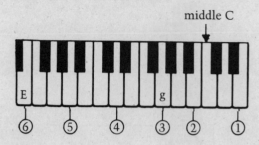

How can you tell when your string is tuned? Well, you are listening for a unison, or identical frequency between your guitar and the reference pitch. Too high or too low and you will hear a bitter or a sour sound. On target, the two instruments melt into one. Best is to tune up the string quickly, going wide on the sharp (high) side, and falling back to the flat (low), then swinging in to the target pitch with smaller errors on each pass. A second hint: listen to the *combined* sound of the instruments. You will hear *beats*, or undulations in the combined wave, that get smoother and finally vanish as you reach the unison.

Now if you have only one tuning fork you will simply set the pitch on one string, and then jockey the others into the correct relationships. This is the most common method of tuning.

Here's how it's done with A as the given pitch.

1. The tuning fork is struck on a soft surface (one's knee cap, for example) and the 5th string is tuned to pitch. (The butt of the vibrating fork may be held between the teeth to free both hands for tuning play.)

2. The 5th string is pinched at the fifth fret (V), giving the note D. The open 4th string is then tuned to D. (You may reach across with the right hand to adjust the tuning while fretting with the left.)

3. Pinch string 4 at V, giving the note G, then tune the open 3rd string to G.

4. Pinch the 3rd string at the *fourth* fret, giving the note B. Tune up the 2nd string.

5. Tune up string 1 using the fifth fret of string 2, then tune string 6 by string 1. Strings 6 and 1 are both E's, but two octaves apart. Summary of unison points:

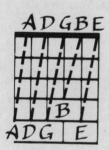

6. Now go back and make sure string 5 is still tuned to A. You may have to repeat the process a couple of times (let new strings stretch for a half hour after an initial tuning or face frustration).

Now try out a few chords—do they sound bright and clear? No? Use your ear to "clear up" the chord, making only slight adjustments. Yes? Congratulations—you are tuned to concert pitch and ready to play.

There are many other ways to tune a guitar. This procedure provides healthy guidelines for the beginner.

Appendix B

Twenty-four Finger Sequences For the Left Hand

1-2-3-4	2-1-3-4	3-1-2-4	4-1-2-3
1-2-4-3	2-1-4-3	3-1-4-2	4-1-3-2
1-3-2-4	2-3-1-4	3-2-1-4	4-2-1-3
1-3-4-2	2-3-4-1	3-2-4-1	4-2-3-1
1-4-2-3	2-4-1-3	3-4-1-2	4-3-1-2
1-4-3-2	2-4-3-1	3-4-2-1	4-3-2-1

For further building of technical strength see: *Ejercicios de Coordinacion Para Guitarra* (Coordination Exercises for Guitar) by Manuel López Ramos; G. Ricordi and Co., 1978, English language version distributed in the USA by Associated Music Publishers, a subsidiary of G. Schirmer, Inc. Maestro Ramos, one of the world's leading concert artists and teachers, here presents an exhaustive group of 120 left-hand combinations in an excellent series of daily exercises.

For further lessons with a South American master see the six progressive lesson books of Julio S. Sagreras, published by Ricordi. The English adaptation by Bernard A. Moore is distributed in the USA by Associated Music Publishers.